Rosemary Conley founded th[...] Grooming organisation in 1972. Eight years later, after developing the business throughout Leicestershire, she sold it to IPC Magazines Ltd and was appointed Managing Director of Successful Slimming Clubs.

Rosemary has written three previous books of which two are specifically on the subject of slimming: *Eat Yourself Slim* and *Eat and Stay Slim*. These publications describe her philosophy that most people trying to lose weight don't eat enough. Her last publication, Positive Living, explains how to succeed at work, at home and at play.

During her time with SAGG and Successful Slimming Clubs, Rosemary has helped around a quarter of a million women to lose weight successfully. She has also devised and scripted two Slimobility exercise cassettes and has appeared on national television and radio programmes.

As a freelance specialist in her subject, Rosemary now works closely with Holiday Inns running Health and Beauty Weekends throughout the United Kingdom, and weekly classes in Holiday Inns in Leicester and Birmingham. She also teaches her philosophy abroad.

Rosemary wrote this book after achieving remarkable results in the reduction of inches from areas of the body she had found impossible to slim. After following a diet prescribed early in 1986 in an attempt to avoid surgery to remove her gall bladder, Rosemary acquired much slimmer hips and thighs. She then developed the diet, based on the nutritional recommendations of her surgeon, and tested it extensively on a team of volunteers. In this book she tells you how it worked for her and her trial team and includes the diet which has been extended to cope with all social needs and personal tastes.

If you follow this diet, you will not only be able to lose unwanted pounds but will see inches disappear from areas you particularly wish to slim.

Rosemary is married and has a daughter, Dawn, by her first marriage. She is also a born-again Christian.

Also in Arrow by Rosemary Conley

EAT YOURSELF SLIM
EAT AND STAY SLIM
POSITIVE LIVING

Rosemary Conley's
HIP AND THIGH DIET

ARROW BOOKS

Arrow Books Limited
62-65 Chandos Place, London WC2N 4NW

An imprint of Century Hutchinson Limited

London Melbourne Sydney Auckland
Johannesburg and agencies throughout
the world

First published 1988
Reprinted 1988 (six times)

Printed and bound in Great Britain by
Anchor Brendon Limited, Tiptree, Essex

ISBN 0 09 954060 6

Acknowledgements

I would like to acknowledge with grateful thanks the help of my Trial Team without whom this book would not have been written.

Special thanks must go to my doctor who helped me through my illness, encouraged me to follow the low-fat diet, and showed so much patience in my defiance of surgery; to my friend Alison Wood for her help in collating the results of the trials; and to my husband Mike for his unfailing support and help throughout both my illness and the production of this book. Thank you all.

Contents

Introduction

'The good old British pear-shape' is anything but funny. Clothes don't fit and all who exhibit such a shape look unsightly in swimwear or shorts. I know because I've been there. Above the waist I could be considered quite slim but below it, ugh. . . !

The good news is that such a figure fault is now a thing of the past and my new diet, having been tested on pear-shaped ladies (and a few men) has proved that we really *can* spot-reduce our bodies, and not just on hips and thighs. My trials produced interesting results in those who wanted to lose weight in other areas too. Those with large busts were able to reduce them. Those with a thick waist discovered a slim one. The results speak for themselves and they are detailed in this book.

As with all great discoveries I hit upon this diet completely by accident. After fifteen years in the slimming business running slimming and exercise clubs, writing books on slimming, and teaching that the only way to lose weight successfully was by counting calories and that if you had heavy hips, or whatever, you were stuck with it, my opinion has been turned upside down. All of what I had said was basically correct but there *are* other ways. You don't have to actually count calories or units or points and you *can* spot-reduce. What a wonderful piece of news I am able to bring to you. I am so excited at the prospect that my diet is going to change the shape and size of so very many people. It will also have the effect of bringing a great deal of personal happiness to those who have genuinely been plagued by this problem of uneven distribution of weight on their body.

This book tells the story of how I discovered the benefits of the diet, how I ran my trials, and the facts about cellulite, exercise and healthy eating. I am confident that you will find the diet amazingly generous and varied – so much so that you won't believe you are actually dieting. The fat tables at the back of the book give the clearest possible guide to food selection and will help to educate you away from fat in your food. Anyone who suffers from high-cholesterol will find this diet very helpful too so long as they take notice of the special list of foods in Chapter 11. There are lots of recipes to choose from so you will never get bored with this diet – in fact I feel sure that before long you will have steered your own and your family's eating habits away from an unhealthy high-fat diet to one of health and vitality.

If this diet worked for all of my volunteers it will work for you. For instance, Mollie Slack lost 2st. 6lbs and with those pounds went 4½ inches off her bust, 7 inches off her waist, 5½ inches from her hips, 7 inches from her widest measurement, 5½ inches off EACH thigh, 2½ inches off each knee and 4 inches from each arm. Another volunteer, Di Driver, slimmed from a size 16 to a size 8! She lost 8 inches from her waist and a staggering 10 inches from her hips! I have 'before' and 'after' photographs to confirm and illustrate the transformation of these ladies.

This book is no confidence trick. The facts included are totally genuine. You will need to follow the diet for a few weeks to see positive results but when you do witness the benefits I promise you you will be as thrilled as I was and as delighted as my trial team. It is worth taking the time to measure yourself periodically to chart your diminishing dimensions and accordingly I have included a measuring chart at the end of this Introduction.

Being overweight and oversized is miserable for anyone. If such a description presently applies to you, follow the advice given in this book and I promise you it will be soon a problem of the past. You've got nothing to lose but your inches and only your health and happiness to gain. Why not make the most of what life now has to offer you, and give it a try.

Measurement Record Chart

Date	Weight	Bust	Waist	Hips	Widest Part	Top of Thighs L	R	Above Knees L	R	Upper Arms L	R	Comments

1
When those inches just disappeared!

Size 10 'Slimfit' jeans – something I never ever dreamed of being able to wear. No one could call me 'Miss Thunder-thighs' any more. It was a miracle. At last my hips and thighs were a normal size.

Ever since I was fifteen I'd had heavy thighs. My mother had heavy thighs and so had my grandmother. I realized there was no alternative but to accept that it was a family legacy from which there was no escape. I dressed around the problem, wearing 'A' line skirts and only wearing trousers if accompanied by a long jacket or sweater. My seat was huge too. It always protruded beyond an acceptable distance no matter what I wore. I hated myself below the waist – and of course as a teacher of slimming and exercise my thighs and bottom were continually on show in all their voluptuous glory in leotards and tights. It was a continual source of embarrassment.

I am sure you can imagine my sheer delight and total surprise when suddenly my body shape changed. This is how it happened:

It was a Saturday in January 1986 and we had invited guests for dinner – friends we hadn't seen for ages so I was determined to spoil them with a special menu. We had avocado and prawn mousse, roast leg of pork, roast potatoes, roast parsnips and other vegetables, Pavlova with lashings of fresh cream and fruit, home-made lemon ice cream, cheese board and biscuits and coffee with cream and after-dinner mints. It was just the kind of meal I love and I relished every mouthful, in fact I think I enjoyed it more than they did!

I continued to consume the left-overs next day. I thought no more about it after the food had disappeared.

I felt generally unwell on Monday, and on Tuesday I woke up with a real ache in my back situated around my kidney area. As I had an important meeting in London which I really had to attend I tried to ignore the pain and hoped that it would go away. It didn't. In fact by the end of the day I felt terribly ill and rushed back to Leicester in time to see my doctor. Since I had recently suffered from a bout of cystitis my doctor suggested that it had developed into a kidney infection and prescribed some medicine.

After two days in bed my condition was worsening. My abdomen was distended and very tender, my body temperature seemed to vary from boiling point to freezing and I just had to call the doctor. He diagnosed a gall bladder infection and prescribed a very strong antibiotic. He very kindly visited me daily for the following five days and advised me to avoid eating fatty foods.

Soon the antibiotics took effect and I felt much better. I returned to work the following Monday but I immediately caught a bad cold and within a day lost my voice completely. Round I went again to my doctor who told me to suck lots of sweets and drink plenty of fluids. How wonderful, I thought. At last I could go and buy lots of sweets with a clear conscience and have a perfect excuse for eating them all day. Glacier mints, glacier fruits, butterscotch – terrific! I loved every mouthful – until later that day when I felt the pain in my back returning. I was panic-stricken. I just couldn't afford to take any more time off work. We were terribly busy and there were my slimming and exercise classes to take too.

Then I realized that it was the butterscotch that had caused the problem. Stupidly I just hadn't thought that it was actually made with butter! I struggled through the rest of the week on a completely fat free diet hoping I could correct the damage, but when I got up on

Saturday morning I felt terrible. Having visisted the bathroom I staggered back to our bedroom and after announcing to Mike how ill I felt I collapsed, eyes wide open, staring into space and motionless. Mike thought I'd died! I came round to hear him dialling 999 and calling an ambulance. I felt like death and kept being terribly sick. Soon the ambulance whisked me off to Leicester Royal Infirmary where I kept passing out and generally causing havoc in the Casualty Department. I felt *so* ill.

I remained in hospital for five days. For two days I couldn't eat much because of all the tests they were doing, but when I did eat anything with the slightest fat content I felt ill again. A variety of tests confirmed two gall stones – a tiny one at the neck of the gall bladder and a slightly larger one at the base of the gall bladder, together with some 'sludge' (sand-size stones). The surgeon said that he could probably operate within the next three weeks and remove my gall bladder and then all my problems would be over and I could eat normally again. He also remarked that this was a common problem among women who were 'fair, fat and forty'. I am fair, I didn't consider myself to be 'fat' but yes, I would be forty next birthday.

What had triggered off the problem was the very high-fat meal I had prepared for my guests at the dinner party. My gall bladder had in effect 'gone on strike' because of the overload I had placed upon it. The function of the gall bladder is to keep the acid and alkali balance in the digestive system. When it stopped working in my case the food inside my digestive system was not being processed properly with the result that it became infected and that was why I was so ill. If I was to avoid surgery I now had to in effect 'pension off' my gall bladder and keep away from foods that would cause it to work hard.

The surgeon was most put out when I said, 'I'm sorry. I don't want to have the operation, but I will stick to the very low fat diet.' I also asked if there was any medication I could take to perhaps dissolve the stones. He was most unimpressed in my stubbornness. It wasn't that I was frightened by the prospect of surgery – I have had four abdominal operations already and survived these without any problems – but I did not particularly want a fifth if it could possibly be avoided. More importantly, I was just winding up one business and about to become self-employed in a new venture in six weeks' time. I wanted to be confined to bed like I wanted a hole in the head! So we agreed to differ and I stuck to my very low fat diet. I felt fine most of the time except if I accidentally ate something fatty, for instance in restaurants where everything seemed to be laced with butter. I have to admit eating out became a nightmare but I coped. I learned quite quickly that food could taste very good without lashings of cream and butter – I used to eat vast quantities of both – providing you went to a little trouble. Yogurt and skimmed milk became best friends and as time went by I felt much more relaxed as I learned which foods were high or low in fat.

I knew I'd lost weight (in fact I had reduced from 8 stone 8 pounds to 8 stone over a period of six weeks). But it was unbelievable how the *inches* had disappeared, particularly from my hips and thighs. I even looked slim in my jodphurs, which I swear are the most unflattering garment ever created. I couldn't believe what I was seeing. My class members continually remarked on the change in my body shape.

They pleaded with me to prepare a diet for them. This I did and it worked. I also put the diet to trial with the general public through BBC's Radio Nottingham and Radio Leicester. It worked for them too. And now it is here for you.

This isn't just another diet. It is a completely new way of reducing inches. There is no need to count calories or fat 'units'. I am sure you will find you lose inches from areas you have previously found impossible to reduce. I have struggled with my weight since my teens for the simple reason that I am a pig! I have an enormous appetite and adore the taste of food. My weight has yo-yo'd from 7 stone 12 pounds to over 10 stone but never ever have I been able to reduce my thighs to their present shape no matter how much weight I lost. My bust always virtually disappeared when I got to 8 stone but not this time – my bust hardly changed. It is that revolting wobbly cellulite at the top of my legs and arms and my huge bottom that have reduced remarkably. All my trousers are baggy around the hips and thighs. I'm thrilled every time I wear my new size 10 slimfit jeans. And the inches have stayed away – even now, over a year later. I can eat loads and I just follow my maintenance programme of minimal fat and moderate portions of good food. And as for my gall stones, after six months my surgeon told me to cease taking the gall bladder medication as I was so much better but to continue with the low fat diet. 'With pleasure,' I replied.

2
The healthiest way to eat

When a smoker dies of lung cancer, the poor victim is almost always blamed for his or her own death. 'It's not surprising she met an early grave, she's smoked forty a day ever since I've known her and that's thirty years,' and, 'What do you expect, smoking all her life – God rest her soul,' are common judgements made by those left behind.

Among many other factors, it is probably true that smoking may be a contributory cause of the disease. But the point is that lung cancer is *immediately* connected with smoking, in everybody's mind.

On the other hand if someone dies of a heart attack it is just accepted that the cause is hereditary, 'He over-exerted himself once too often,' or most commonly, it was 'Just bad luck'. We have not yet been sufficiently educated to realize that the risk of dying from the greatest killer disease in the Western world could be drastically reduced if only we took preventative measures by eating sensibly and looking after our bodies. The earlier we take these steps the better for everyone concerned.

One in four deaths in this country is caused by heart disease. This year over 200,000 people will die from heart disease; that's Wembley stadium filled to capacity four times over! No other condition claims so many lives – yet how many people really know what risks they run? If you were to ask twenty men or women in the street what they should do to avoid heart disease the majority would say, 'take more exercise and eat margarine instead of butter.' We are, in reality, extremely ignorant of the various causes of this greatest killer disease.

Whilst there are many types of heart disease, the most common and the most tragic is the type that causes heart attacks and is called coronary heart disease. Here's how it comes about:

Most of us have seen a heart in one form or another, whether on television or in school or even at the butchers. The human heart is about the size of a fist and is a muscle filled with blood. It contracts about seventy times a minute pumping blood around our body. The heart needs a constant good supply of oxygen which it gets from the bloodstream. However, the heart's own oxygen supply is not taken from the blood which is continually being pumped through it to service the rest of the body, but from separate little arteries which are called coronary arteries. These branch off from the main artery, called the aorta, and then divide into lots of smaller branches which are all over the surface of the heart.

The problems start in early adult life when the walls of these coronary arteries become 'furred up' and narrower. The narrowing is caused by a fatty deposit called atheroma and if it gets too thick and the coronary arteries too narrow, the blood supply to the heart becomes restricted or even blocked. This condition is called 'coronary heart disease'.

The disease has two main forms, angina and heart attack. Angina occurs when the coronary arteries have become narrower very gradually and is only noticed when the heart has to work harder than usual. The symptoms of angina are a heavy cramp-like pain across the chest which can spread to the neck, shoulder, arm and even the jaw. Angina is quite different from a heart attack because it is usually relieved by a short period of rest or relaxation. It can also be relieved or controlled by drugs and in severe cases, surgery.

On the other hand a heart attack occurs when there

is a sudden and severe blockage in one of the coronary arteries so that the blood supply to part of the heart is actually cut off. The blockage is usually caused by a blood clot forming in an artery already narrowed by fatty atheroma. This is called a coronary thrombosis or just 'a coronary'. In some cases the effects of the blockage can be so severe that the heart stops beating altogether and this is called a cardiac arrest. Unless the heart starts beating again within a few minutes the person will die, and in fifty per cent of all fatal heart attacks the victim dies within thirty minutes.

The pain is a crushing vice-like ache felt in the chest. It can also spread to the neck, arm or jaw and doesn't usually ease off for several hours. Sickness, giddiness and feelings of faintness often accompany the pain.

There are many factors which affect our vulnerability to heart disease. As well as our family history, sex and age, we must also consider how physically active we are, the amount of stress we have to endure, whether or not we smoke, what we eat and, very importantly, whether or not we are overweight.

Before I go on to talk about the diet and overweight issue let us first consider the other factors that can cause heart disease.

People who have a family history of heart disease are undoubtedly at greater risk. It is obvious that they should take *particular* care to follow preventative guide-lines to reduce their risk to a minimum. There is no doubt that the older we get the greater is the risk of suffering a heart attack. The narrowing of the arteries which can lead to angina and heart attacks tends to increase with age. Men are more at risk from heart disease than women. In fact a man in his late forties is five times more likely to die of heart disease than a woman of the same age. But it would be a mistake for women to consider themselves reasonably 'safe', because after the menopause a woman loses the protective effect of her hormones and her chances of suffering from heart disease are almost equal to a man's. In recent years there has in fact been an increased incidence of heart disease in women in their thirties and forties.

Apart from age, sex and family history, the other contributory factors are voluntary so the choice really is ours!

Cigarette smoking can double our risk of dying from a heart attack and heavy smokers are even more likely to die young. For instance a man who is over fifty and who smokes over twenty cigarettes a day is *four* times more likely to suffer from heart disease than a non-smoker of the same age. Women smokers are at just as much risk as men and at even greater risk if over the age of thirty-five and on the pill. The answer here must be to give up smoking – as soon as you do, you begin to reduce the risk of a heart attack. And the good news is that you could be almost back to a non-smoker's risk level within a few years. Cutting down or smoking low tar cigarettes will not protect you against heart disease.

The reason cigarette smoking adversely affects the heart is because the nicotine in tobacco smoke increases the blood pressure. This is because the carbon monoxide content of cigarette smoke cuts down the amount of oxygen in the blood and accordingly the heart has to work harder yet it is getting less oxygen. Smoking also speeds up the 'furring up' of the arteries in the heart. Smoking is bad news from every direction – from being damaging to your health and the health of those around you to being smelly and totally antisocial.

A great deal of heart disease could also be prevented if everyone over the age of thirty-five had their blood pressure checked every few years by their doctor. Blood pressure is the pressure which the heart and arteries apply in order to squeeze the blood around the body. When we are sitting or resting our blood pressure remains at a steady resting level. This level increases depending on our activity and the demand for a surge of blood to be sent where it is needed, for instance to the muscles during exercise or to our brain when under pressure mentally. As soon as we stop exerting ourselves the blood pressure returns to normal again.

Hypertension, or high blood pressure, is when the resting blood pressure is higher than normal. Whilst high blood pressure is rare among young people it is common among those over thirty-five, no doubt caused by following an unhealthy lifestyle – eating too much, consuming too much alcohol, having too much salt in our food, smoking, lack of exercise, and suffering from too much stress. Unfortunately most people have no idea that they have high blood pressure because it doesn't actually *feel* any different. But high blood pressure makes the heart work harder resulting in heart disease. There is also the danger of a stroke which is when a blood clot occurs in the brain and the blood supply is cut off.

The good news is that blood pressure can be helped enormously by reducing your weight to its correct level, by not drinking too much alcohol, by stopping smoking, eating less salt, increasing the amount of exercise and by learning to relax.

Stress and anxiety are often self-inflicted. I believe that every problem can be resolved, and that if it can be approached sensibly and thoughtfully, it can even be turned to advantage. If ignored, stress not only contributes to physical disorders such as heart disease, high blood pressure, ulcers and asthma, it can also lead to a variety of mental illnesses of which insomnia, depression and irritability are just early symptoms. On the other hand, if we are under-stressed we will become lethargic and tired and psychosomatic illnesses could occur. A certain amount of stress, therefore, is an essential part of our everyday life. It keeps us on our toes.

Whilst exercise is regularly advocated as essential to a healthy heart this recommendation is often misunderstood. If an overweight man in his fifties who is a heavy smoker, has a family history of heart disease and is working in a stressful job were to decide to 'get fit' and invite a colleague for a game of squash for the first time in twenty years, he would be doing just about the best he could to give himself a heart attack. His heart just would not be able to cope with the strain. The heart will benefit most from the kind of exercise that builds up stamina – the ability to keep going without gasping for breath. Stamina depends on the efficiency of our muscles and circulation and of course the most important muscle of all is the heart itself.

Regular moderate exercise such as brisk walking is the answer for the gentleman described above. As he becomes fitter he may be able to do more and more, but moderation is the key factor. Playing golf or walking the dog is ideal exercise for anyone and the fresh air will be beneficial too. In order to build stamina something more energetic like swimming, cycling or keeping fit to music can be very beneficial and enjoyable. Regular exercise of this kind improves the balance of fatty substances in the blood stream, lowers the resting blood pressure level and strengthens the heart muscle. But whatever it is we decide to do, it must be continued in the long term. A mad spurt of extreme physical activity for two weeks a year will do us nothing but harm. It is therefore essential to find a form of activity we enjoy so that we are happy to practise it two or three times a week and continue it for life.

So now to the problem of obesity. Obesity can also increase the risk of heart disease, not in itself but because of the many other conditions it can create, conditions which most certainly *do* contribute to heart disease (high blood pressure and diabetes are the most common). The more overweight you are the more likely you are to get high blood pressure and diabetes. Often members of my slimming classes have been referred to me by their doctors, anxious for their patients to reduce their weight and so help reduce their blood pressure. As soon as they lose weight their blood pressure returns to normal.

Don't forget it is not just ourselves we are putting at risk. If we serve bad-for-you foods at home we affect our own hearts, certainly, but worse still, we are serving the wrong food to our families. We have their hearts in our hands too.

There is little doubt that to have become obese in the first instance we have simply eaten too much of the wrong sorts of foods. In other words, too many fatty and sugary foods which are positively loaded with calories – bread spread with lashings of butter, an abundance of fried foods, cream cakes, biscuits, chocolate, crisps and so on. The types of foods overweight people love.

The fat in our food is not only responsible for the extra inches on our hips. It can also push up our blood cholesterol level. (See chapter 11 for list of foods high in cholesterol.) Cholesterol is a natural substance in the blood and is mostly made from the fat in the food we eat, though the body itself is quite capable of making an adequate supply. If there is a lot of fat in our diet we have a high cholesterol level. This can have the effect of accelerating the build-up of atheroma which in turn eventually leads to heart disease. Therefore the higher the level of cholesterol in the blood the greater the risk of problems with the heart.

There has been so much talk of saturated and unsaturated fats that most people have heard of them. Few, however, actually understand what they are. The difference between the two types is their chemical make-up and whilst I don't want to go into lengthy explanations about the proportions of carbon and hydrogen atoms that determine the types of fatty acid it is important to realize that fat isn't just a single compound but comes in many forms. All fats are made up of fatty acids: some of these are saturated fatty acids (called saturates), the rest are unsaturated and these include a special group called polyunsaturated fatty acids (or polyunsaturates). Different fats have different proportions of various fatty acids. Most are high in saturates but some are high in polyunsaturates.

As far as the heart is concerned saturates are considered the main enemy. If we eat too much food high in saturates it can increase our blood cholesterol level and that in turn increases our risk of heart disease. Saturated fat is to be found mostly in animal products like cream, butter, eggs, offal, and in the fat on meat and poultry. In place of butter or margarine, alternatives such as Flora are recommended as it is high in polyunsaturates.

It would be a mistake to *increase* the consumption of foods high in polyunsaturates in the belief that they will 'do us good'. We must, after all, remember that we can produce sufficient cholesterol within our own bodies and that fats high in polyunsaturates contain the same amount of calories as the original saturated products so they do not aid slimming in any way.

So this now leaves us with the view that if we reduce our intake of *all* fat our health will certainly benefit and so will our waistlines. And whilst it is impossible to state categorically that heart disease can be caused by eating too much fat, in recent investigations it was observed that among the groups of people who consumed high amounts of fat the incidence of heart attack was far higher than among those who followed a low fat diet. It would be easy to conclude from this research that fat can actually cause heart disease but with so many other factors to be taken into consideration it is impossible to make such a simple statement. However, it *is* generally acknowledged that to reduce the consumption of fat in our daily diet will almost certainly reduce the risk of heart disease along with other medical conditions.

So how much fat do we actually need? The average consumption of fat in the Western world at the present time is about 130 grams (over 4½ ounces) a day per person. This fat includes everything from the obvious fats like butter and oil to those hidden in cakes, biscuits and fried foods. The amount of fat we actually *need* is staggeringly low at 5 grams (less than a quarter of an ounce) per day, providing it contains the right kind of fatty acids. As I do not suggest or recommend that we reduce our intake to such a very low level, we need not concern ourselves that we will eat insufficient quantities to endanger our health. However, it is clear that currently far too much fat is consumed and it is an ideal area in which to make a significant reduction without fear of nutrient deficiency.

So to sum up, if we want to help ourselves towards a healthy heart and a long and happy life we need to eat a low fat diet, take regular exercise and stop smoking. If we can reduce our weight to around that of our youth and eat well enough to give us the energy to work and live our lives to the full, we will all benefit. In addition, we will make our GPs very happy!

3
Tried and tested

All my adult life I had adored foods which were high in fat. In fact I had never even imagined life without fat so it was something of a challenge to create a very low fat diet for myself, first of all, and then for my slimmers – a diet which at the same time as being very low in fat included all the necessary nutrients.

Butter, margarine and oil are obviously high in fat – in fact they are 99% fat. Foods like eggs, avocado pears and peanuts are not so easily recognizable. But first let's get everything into understandable perspective.

In the last chapter I said that the average consumption of fat in the Western world is about 130 grams (over 4½ ounces) a day. So, 130 grams of fat is equal to almost 5 ounces of butter. 'But I don't eat anywhere *near* that amount of fat in a day,' I hear you say, and of course in the form of butter or pure fat, no doubt you don't. You probably eat only one ounce or even half that! So how do we eat the rest of our daily intake of fat? Of course it's the cheese, milk, eggs, meat, fried foods, cakes, pastries, pies, nuts, cream, ice cream, mayonnaise, sauces . . . the list is endless. What foods are left, then, which contain no fat or at least very little? At first it is difficult to think of anything except apples and oranges!

I prepared a diet as free from fat as possible yet incorporating protein, carbohydrate, vitamins and minerals. In formulating the diet I paid particular attention to moisture, realizing that, after all, the inclusion of fat in our daily diet added considerably to its palatability.

I also tried to incorporate a strong element of freedom so that a long term eating habit could be created. I didn't want anyone to feel that this diet was a 'prison sentence' to be endured for a few weeks or months before old habits could be reintroduced. No, this was a new healthy way of eating that was going to change previous diet failures into long term success stories. It could also help towards healthier generations in the future. After all, the way we feed our children has a great bearing on how they will eat in later life and in turn how *they* will feed *their* families in years to come.

I first gave the diet to some of the members at my classes. Not only did they enjoy it but it certainly worked extremely well for those that followed it properly. However, as they had mostly lost significant amounts of weight already and it hadn't occurred to me to ask them to measure their weekly progress in terms of inches, the results, whilst remarkable, were only visual. I still needed evidence in black and white that the inches really *did* disappear from areas previously impossible to reduce – namely the hips and thighs.

As a regular broadcaster on local radio I went along to Radio Nottingham for one of my phone-ins on slimming. It seemed like a good idea to ask for 'guinea pigs' to test the diet. They were asked to monitor their progress not only with scales but with a tape measure. One hundred ladies kindly volunteered and eight weeks later I asked them to complete a lengthy questionnaire. I received twenty completed record sheets – and a load of very apologetic letters explaining why the remainder had been unable to do justice to the trial. Reasons from holidays, family and work problems, moving house, and so on were given. Nevertheless, the twenty who *did* reply offered most interesting statistics, observations and confirmation of the effectiveness of the diet.

At this stage I felt I had actually discovered something more than just another diet. On the questionnaires there were comments such as: 'It was a very nice diet, the first that has actually worked for me all over my body! I have more confidence and feel good in clothes again. Thank you.' And, 'the "Bum and Thigh" diet *does* work! I shall certainly be interested in carrying on with it as part of my natural diet now. Thank you.' Another said, 'I have been thoroughly happy with this diet, though I must admit I do enjoy bread, fruit and salads in the normal way of things. There was very little inconvenience in leaving out the butter and salad cream, and I have enjoyed the diet even more whilst watching the inches disappear, and enjoying being complimented on how much slimmer I look. Oh, and how lovely to be able to open the wardrobe doors and say 'I haven't got anything to wear – they are all *too big*.' Absolute Heaven! Very many thanks.'

I was beginning to realize that this diet could in fact be a breakthrough for all those who were still left with the typical British 'pear' shape, even after losing weight successfully. However, I felt we still needed more trials so that I could prove without doubt that my inch loss theory worked.

I was holding a slimming exhibition at the beginning of September at the Holiday Inn, Leicester, and wanted as much publicity as possible to attract visitors. I rang my friends at Radio Leicester and Peter Crankshaw, the producer of the 'phone-in programme *Cross Talk* said 'Yes' to my suggestion that I mention my exhibition. I also told him about the new hip and thigh diet and said I could do with some more volunteers to try it out. This all seemed ideal from everyone's point of view so the following week I went along.

The programme was being broadcast from Radio Leicester's shop in Leicester's Haymarket shopping precinct. Morgan Cross, the presenter, and I chatted about my new diet and the telephone lines immediately came alive. I discussed the format of the diet with various callers and then one of my members came in to the shop. Di Driver had been coming to my classes for some time and she knew I was appearing on the programme but I had no idea that she planned on paying me a visit 'on air'. In fact I was quite embarrassed by her arrival as I was aware that listeners might think I had invited her. I honestly hadn't. Her visit was spontaneous, she said, and her testimony on air really said it all. She had lost three stones in four months and had extremely slim hips and thighs to prove it. You would never have believed that she had ever had a problem in that area. Well, volunteers for the diet seemed to be coming out of the woodwork! People were coming over to us out of shops, pleading to be included in my trials. The 'phones just didn't stop ringing. We gave my home address over the air so that volunteers could send me a stamped, self-addressed envelope so that I could forward them a diet sheet. It was just as well I did request an s.a.e. as over the next ten days I received over five hundred requests!

My husband Mike and I spent the whole of the following week opening mail, printing diet sheets and letters of instruction and stuffing envelopes. The names and addresses of every volunteer had to be entered on to our computer. Our village Post Office had never seen so much activity!

It was all a lot of fun and of course very encouraging. There were lots of letters of weight history and dietary abnormalities which had to be considered. Various questions had to be answered. It was a major operation.

The wide area covered by the enquiries was amazing. I had letters which started, 'We were travelling up the motorway from London to Glasgow and I heard you . . .' or 'I live in Devon but I was staying in Leicester when I heard you. Please can I . . . ?' It was tremendous to get such a positive response.

I gave out my home address to save Radio Leicester having to handle the enquiries. That address is The Old Parsonage, Mountsorrel, Leicester, LE12 7AT. Here are some of the varieties of addresses which still managed to find us. I do hope the senders do not mind my reproducing them, but they certainly brightened Mike's and my days as we slogged through the sorting and despatching process: Neils Parsonage, The Old Bakehouse, The Old Partridge, The Old Parsnip.

My name received a variety of treatments too. Here is a sample: Rosemary Garther, Rosemary Collenage, Rosemary Colledge, Rosemary Collins, Rosemary Cullis and Valerie Connolly. I was also charmed that one lady called me Rosemary Clooney!

I emphasized to the volunteers that this was a trial and they were now a member of my trial 'team'. If they felt they could not follow the diet or didn't want to be committed I asked them to please return all the papers, and about seventy of them did just that.

Eight weeks later the questionnaires were sent out and again about 20 per cent responded with completed details. There was another pile too, giving reasons why the remainder could not complete the eight week trial. Nevertheless, I now had 120 people, 116 women and 4 men, who had followed the diet for a full eight-week period.

I was delighted and surprised that all 120 volunteers had lost weight, with losses varying from 3 pounds to 1 stone 12 pounds during the eight-week trial. An amazing 98 of them stated they had lost inches from areas they had considered difficult to slim or had found impossible to reduce previously. Needless to say I was staggered at this result. Thirty-one of my trial team had never previously attempted to slim yet 25 of them said they lost inches from areas they considered a real problem and particularly wanted to reduce. In the end only 11 per cent said they did not particularly lose more inches than previous dieting attempts had produced.

I was also overwhelmed by the tremendously encouraging comments made by my trial team. Here are just a few.

Mrs A. W. wrote: 'I would like to take this opportunity

to thank you for the time and effort you have put into compiling this diet which has made a bigger difference to my weight and dimensions than any other diet I have been on. . . . '

Mrs J. P. wrote: 'I am very pleased with the results of the diet. It took me about ten days to work my way into it, after that I found it very acceptable. I feel great! My stomach has flattened. Buttocks have been a problem for years and now they are greatly reduced. I am very grateful to you. . . . '

Mrs V. W. wrote: 'Very easy to follow. Most important was losing inches off my hips, which I haven't been able to do before. . . . '

Another Mrs V. W. wrote: 'Many thanks for the diet sheet. I feel a different woman! I have angina which is very unpleasant but I can move about more easily since losing a bit of weight and I used to suffer every night with heartburn but since having no fat I can honestly say I haven't suffered at all. . . . It's lovely to get into a size 16 instead of size 20. . . . '

Mr B. P. reported that he had already lost 3 stone some time before but had stuck at 15 stone and was pleased when he started to lose again. 'Everyone has remarked on how I have slimmed in all the right places.'

Volunteers were asked to measure weekly their bust, waist, hips, widest body measurement, (usually around lower hips/tops of thighs), each thigh, each knee and each arm. The results were collated and several quite unexpected facts emerged.

Some lost many inches but comparatively little weight and nearly everyone lost inches off their 'fattest' part. This is unusual as with most other diets slimmers often complain of 'losing it from the parts I want to keep', usually the bust. The results showed that only twelve volunteers lost 3 inches or more from their bust and all but two of these had measurements of 40 inches or more prior to following my diet. The other two had measured 39 inches and 39½ inches respectively and both were delighted to have reduced their bust size. Inch loss from others varied according to their size but those with a 34–36 inch bust measurement either lost nothing at all or only an inch or an inch and a half. The risk of losing what little bust they might have is enough to discourage many an overweight lady from commencing to diet, so this diet must therefore be good news for them.

Another interesting factor was that not only did hips and thighs diminish but waist measurements reduced amazingly too. The league table for parts of the body to benefit most looks like this:

Hips	52%
Thighs	43%
Waist	29%
Tummy	16%
Arms	16%
Bust	9%
Knees	3%
Other	3%

N.B. More than one part of the body was stated by some volunteers.

The number of inches lost from the various areas varied enormously, as did the weight losses. A representative sample of case histories follows.

Sex	Age	Height	Weight	Bust inches	Waist inches	Hips inches	Wide inche
F.1	51	5 ft 4 ins					
At commencement			11 st 0 lbs	42	30	41¾	42
After 8 weeks			9 st 12 lbs	38	27½	38	39
Total weight/inches lost			1 st 2 lbs	4	2½	3¾	3
F.2*	49	5 ft 8½ ins	12 st 9 lbs	39½	35	43	45
After 8 weeks			12 st 1 lbs	38	32	41	42
After 16 weeks			11 st 2 lbs	37	30	39	40
After 30 weeks			10 st 3 lbs	35	28	37½	38
Total weight/inches lost			2 st 6 lbs	4½	7	5½	7
F.3	79	5 ft 7½ ins	12 st 2 lbs	39	34	42½	44½
After 8 weeks			11 st 3 lbs	35½	31½	40	41
Total weight/inches lost			13 lbs	3½	2½	2½	3½

| Thighs inches | | Knees inches | | Arms inches | | Noticeable inch loss from areas previously difficult to slim: |
L.	R.	L.	R.	L.	R.	
1½	21¾	14¼	14½	11½	12	
20	20	13¾	14	10¾	11	Hips
1½	1¾	½	½	¾	1	
26	26	17½	17½	14	14	
2½	23	16	16	12	11	
22	22	15½	15½	11	11	Tummy and thighs
0½	20½	15	15	10	10	
5½	5½	2½	2½	4	4	
24	25	19	19½	12½	13	
23	24	16	15½	12½	13	Waist, hips and thighs
1	1	3	4	–	–	

Sex	Age	Height	Weight	Bust inches	Waist inches	Hips inches	Wi... inc...
F.4*	17	5 ft 4½ ins	9 st 6 lbs	35	29½	35½	3...
After 8 weeks			8 st 10 lbs	35	28	34½	34...
After 16 weeks			8 st 4 lbs	35	25½	32½	3...
Total inches/weight lost			1 st 2 lbs	0	4	3	
F.5	32	4 ft 11½ ins	10 st 2 lbs	39	29½	40	4...
After 8 weeks			9 st 13 lbs	37	28	38	3...
Total weight/inches lost			3 lbs	2	1½	2	
F.6	63	4 ft 10 ins	10 st 0 lbs	38	32	41	4...
After 8 weeks			9 st 6 lbs	35¼	29	38	3...
Total weight/inches lost			8 lbs	2¾	3	3	
F.7	56	5 ft 1½ ins	11 st 7 lb	44	40	44	4...
After 8 weeks			11 st 1 lb	38½	37	39	3...
Total weight/inches lost			6 lbs	5½	3	5	

Thighs inches L.	Thighs inches R.	Knees inches L.	Knees inches R.	Arms inches L.	Arms inches R.	Noticeable inch loss from areas previously difficult to slim:
22½	22½	14½	14½	10½	10½	
21	21	14	14	10	10	
20	20	14	14	9½	9½	Waist, hips and thighs
2½	2½	½	½	1	1	
22½	23	18½	18½	13	13	
20	20	15	15	11	11	Arms and legs
2½	3	3½	3½	2	2	
25	25	19	19	12¼	12¼	
23	23	16	16	11½	11½	Hips and thighs
2	2	3	3	¾	¾	
20½	20½	15	15	14	14	
18¾	19	14½	14½	13¼	13¼	Bust, waist and hips
1¾	1½	½	½	¾	¾	

Sex	Age	Height	Weight	Bust inches	Waist inches	Hips inches	Wid... inch...
F.8	34	5 ft 3½ ins	10 st 7 lbs	36	35	39	42
After 8 weeks			9 st 5 lbs	34½	30	37½	39½
Total weight/inches lost			1 st 2 lbs	1½	5	1½	2
F.9	38	5 ft 6 ins	12 st 0 lbs	40	31	42	42
After 8 weeks			10 st 10 lbs	37	29	38½	38
Total lost			1 st 4 lbs	3	2	3½	3
F.10	45	5 ft 3 ins	12 st 8 lbs	46	40	42½	46
After 8 weeks			11 st 7 lbs	43½	36	40½	42
Total loss			1 st 1 lbs	2½	4	2	4
F.11	39	5 ft 9 ins	14 st 13 lbs	38	37	45	46
After 8 weeks			13 st 7 lbs	36	32	42½	43
Total lost			1 st 6 lbs	2	5	2½	?
F.12	40	5 ft 4 ins	11 st 0 lbs	36	31	41	43
After 8 weeks			10 st 0 lbs	35	28½	39	41
Total lost			1 st 0 lbs	1	2½	2	2

Thighs inches L.	R.	Knees inches L.	R.	Arms inches L.	R.	Noticeable inch loss from areas previously difficult to slim:
24	23¾	16¼	16	11¾	11½	
22	22	15	15	11	11¼	Tummy, waist and hips
2	1¾	1¼	1	¾	½	
25	24½	17	17	12	12½	
2½	21½	15¾	16	11	11½	Not stated
2½	3	1¼	1	1	1	
5½	25½	16½	16½	14	14	
23	23	15½	16	12½	12½	Arms and waist
2½	2½	1	½	1½	1½	
28	27	20	20	14	14	
25	25	19	19	13	13	Hips, legs and arms
3	2	1	1	1	1	
5½	25½	17	17¼	11¼	11½	
23	23½	15¼	15½	10½	10½	Hips, thighs and legs
2½	2	1¾	1¾	¾	1	

Sex	Age	Height	Weight	Chest inches	Waist inches	Hips inches	Wid inch
M.13 63		Not stated	14 st 6 lbs	42½	45	44½	–
After 8 weeks			13 st 4 lbs	40	43½	42	–
Total lost			1 st 2 lbs	2½	1½	2½	–
M.14 48		5 ft 11 ins	15 st 0 lbs	44½	42½	45¾	–
After 8 weeks			14 st 0 lbs	43½	41	44½	–
Total weight/inches lost			1 st 0 lbs	1	1½	1¼	–
M.15 21		5 ft 9 ins	14 st 2 lbs	41½	38	39½	41
After 8 weeks			13 st 2 lbs	38½	36	38½	38
Total weight/inches lost			1 st 0 lbs	3	2	1	
M.16 63		5 ft 7 ins	14 st 10 lbs	46	44	43	4
After 8 weeks			13 st 8 lbs	41	41	41	4
Total weight/inches lost			1 st 2 lbs	5	3	2	

| Thighs inches | | Knees inches | | Arms inches | | Noticeable inch loss from areas previously difficult to slim: |
L.	R.	L.	R.	L.	R.	
23	23	15½	15½	14½	15	
21	22	15	15	14	13½	
2	1	½	½	½	1½	
22½	23½	16¾	17½	13¼	13½	
21	22	16½	17½	13	13½	Midriff and stomach
1½	1½	¼	–	¼	–	
26	25	17	17	15	14	
24½	24	16	16	14½	14	
1½	1	1	1	½	–	
26	26	17	17	14	14	
22½	23	15¼	15¼	13	13	Stomach and waist
3½	3	1¾	1¾	1	1	

Sex	Age	Height	Weight	Bust inches	Waist inches	Hips inches	Wid inch
F.17	33	5 ft 5 ins	15 st 0 lbs	43	40	49	5ⁿ
After 8 weeks			13 st 2 lbs	39	34	42½	45
Total weight/inch loss			1 st 12 lbs	4	6	6½	6

* Members of the original Nottingham trial team who had kept me informe

Thighs inches		Knees inches		Arms inches		Noticeable inch loss from areas previously difficult to slim:
L.	R.	L.	R.	L.	R.	
28	27	20	19½	15	15	
24	25	16½	17	12	13	Arms, hips, bust and thighs
4	2	3½	2½	3	2	

progress beyond the eight week period.

Because some of the volunteers subsequently joined my slimming and exercise classes which I hold weekly at the Holiday Inn in Leicester, I was able to hear first hand the kind of encouraging comments which only served to confirm what I was seeing with my eyes as each week passed. Di Driver brought along some photographs taken just over a year ago. She looked very 'hippy' in her denim jeans – a typical British pear shape. She lost three stone on the low fat diet and reduced from a size 16 to a size 8! Whilst she hadn't completed a weekly measurement chart she had kept a personal record of her waist and hip measurement. She had lost 8 inches off her waist and a staggering 10 inches off her hips over a period of seven months. Her 'after' photographs portrayed a very very different shaped lady – one you would not have believed could ever have been pear shaped.

Rose Mundy told me of her continual battle with overweight thighs, a problem that had been with her for as long as she could remember. Rose, now 66, explained that she used to visit the doctor regularly as her thighs would continually rub against each other and actually bleed because they were so big. She used to carry pads of cotton wool to dress the wounds from the chafing. She tried all kinds of diets and even when she stuck rigidly to an Energen 1000 Calories a Day diet and lost over two stone not a single inch went from her thighs. The doctor offered Rose slimming tablets to help her lose even more weight but he said he was not very hopeful that she would lose it from her legs. He told her, 'Some people are blessed with more weight in some areas than others. Those parts are usually the most difficult to slim and as yet there is no diet to slim down specific problem areas.' When Rose's sister heard my broadcast on Radio Leicester she immediately rang Rose to tell her. The following week Rose came along to my class with her sister and started the diet immediately. It was two months later that she told me of her problem and the

44

discomfort it had previously caused her. She proudly showed me the size 16 slacks she was wearing – eight weeks earlier she had been wearing size 22! She had lost 2½ inches from each thigh, 3 inches from her hips and 3 inches off her waist. She had lost only 1 inch off her 39 inch bust. She said she felt a different woman. 'Imagine,' she said, beaming, 'for the first time in my life I can walk down the road without my legs even touching – it's absolutely marvellous.'

Pat Bavester was another person for whom the low fat diet worked where others had failed. Pat had been attending my classes for a long time – years in fact. Not because she couldn't lose weight but because she enjoyed coming along for a weekly work-out session and it helped to keep her weight in check. Pat always reminded me of my own shape – a reasonably well proportioned figure but very heavy on the hips and thighs. As soon as I had the diet ready for issue at the classes, Pat was first on my mental list of people who I hoped would particularly benefit. And sure enough, within a few weeks the inches disappeared. Pat couldn't believe the comments she was receiving from people who noticed the marked difference in her shape. 'Haven't you lost loads of weight!' they would say, though in fact she had only lost 6 pounds. However she lost 1½ inches from each thigh and 2 inches from her hips, and she can now wear size 12 clothes instead of size 16. Apparently she had had heavy thighs all her life and still cannot get used to her new shape. 'It's really wonderful,' she says.

Perhaps the most remarkable inch loss of all was from Mollie Slack, one of my early volunteers from Radio Nottingham. Mollie would send me a regular bulletin of her progress and since May 1986 she had reduced her weight from 12 stone 9 pounds to 10 stone 3 pounds (a loss of 2 stone 6 pounds). Her bust has reduced from 39½ inches to 35 inches (a loss of 4½ inches), her waist from 35 inches to 28 inches (7 inches) her hips from 43 inches to 37½ inches (5½ inches) and her widest part (around the lower hips and thighs) had reduced by 7 inches from 45 inches to 38 inches. But perhaps the most staggering inch loss of all was from her thighs which have reduced by an amazing 5½ inches each! Her knees have slimmed by 2½ inches each and her arms by 4 inches each. Now when you think of the comparatively small measurement of a single limb, the inch loss is truly amazing. Mollie can't believe her new shape and tells me that her colleagues can't get over the transformation either. Recently at an important business function several of the managers from the company for whom she works came over to take a closer look. 'You look twenty years younger since you've lost that weight,' – and it was more than one that said it too! Mollie had always been heavy, even as a teenager, so as she approached her fiftieth birthday she said 'it's good to feel better and younger than ever'.

Another Nottingham volunteer, Sue, said, 'I may not have lost a lot in pounds but it's great to know I can lose inches from parts I didn't think I could ever reduce.' Sue lost only 3 pounds but lost 2½ and 3 inches off her thighs and an amazing 3½ inches from just above her knees!

Another lady who asked not to be named sent me her measurement sheet as well as the completed questionnaire. Her comments alongside her weekly measuring sessions said so much that I felt you would enjoy reading them too:

Week 1: 2 pounds lost. ½ inch off my bust, 1 inch off my waist and ½ inch off my hips. 2 inches from the girth round my tum, nothing from my legs but ¼ inch off each arm. A good week. Feel less sluggish and taking 15 minutes exercise each day.
Week 2: 3 pounds off this week. Only ½ inch from my waist, another inch from my tum but no change elsewhere. My feet have reduced by one size! Feeling

better but where has the 5 lbs gone from? Don't feel any slimmer!

Week 3: Another pound gone, ¼ inch off my bust, ¼ inch from my waist and ⅜ inch off my hips but another inch off my tum! Measurements of limbs remain unchanged. 'Only a pound this week – not eaten too much as I've had a very sore throat and cold.

Week 4: 1½ pounds gone and another ¼ inch from my bust and waist but a whole inch off my hips. Another ¾ from my tum and whilst my thighs and knees remain the same I've lost ¼ inch off each arm. Terrible day – just wanted to eat and eat. Controlled it by eating fruit – no gain in weight. [Next day] Feel SO MUCH BETTER! Cold gone – great!! What a difference a day makes.

Week 5: Only ½ pound weight lost but another ½ inch from my bust and ¼ inch from my hips. Everything else stays the same. Look and feel better – stepping out – inches *are* going!'

Week 6: Gained a pound. ½ inch on my bust measurement, ½ inch on my waist and hips, also my tum. However, ¼ inch off each knee and 1 inch from one arm and ½ inch off the other. Went away for half-term holiday.

Week 7: Lost 1 pound and the ½ inch off my bust. ¼ inch goes from my waist, hips remain unchanged but 2 inches from my tum. ½ inch goes from my thighs and ¾ inch from each knee. Arms remain unchanged. Walk so much more briskly. One more week to go. Feel better – not bloated.

Week 8: Another pound gone, ½ inch off my bust (now 40½ inches) ¾ inch from my waist, 1 inch off my hips, tum remains the same but have lost 5 inches already, no more off thighs but another ¼ inch off my knees and arms remain unchanged. Love this diet – part of my life now.

This lady only lost ½ inch from her thighs. She lost ¼ inch from each knee and ¾ inch from each arm. It was intesting that when she started her thighs only measured 21½ inches which is slim by comparison with most of the other volunteers. On the other hand her measurement around her tum was 44 inches and from here she lost 5 inches. Her bust reduced from 42½ inches to 40½ inches, her waist from 36½ inches to 34½ inches and her hips from 42½ inches to 40 inches. Again we see that inches are lost from the areas most in need of reduction. This lady also added, 'My tum is so much flatter – feel much more in control of my body. I don't feel bloated. I always have a problem to lose weight and have problems with many 'E' additives which I have sorted out. This is just my kind of diet – no junk food, plenty of fruit which I love. Sincerely and Thank you . . . Mrs X.'

I could fill a book with the other similar comments which were written on the questionnaires but I think we can take it as read that the trials proved beyond doubt that if you followed the diet moderately strictly you could definitely lose inches from parts usually untouched by normal dieting methods. So the choice really is yours at the end of the day. . . !

4
Your good health!

Apart from the obvious benefits to those who, like myself, suffer with gall stones, I was surprised to read so many other benefits to health that had been enjoyed by many volunteers.

A lady who suffers with a hiatus hernia wrote, 'I have had to take Rennies after meals for years but since I have been on this diet I haven't had a Rennie for five weeks! It's great.' Another commented that she didn't suffer heartburn any more. There were many who commented on improved digestion. Perhaps the most general comment in this direction was the fact that many felt far less bloated and felt their mobility had consequently benefitted. Said one gentleman, 'I have felt a lot better in myself. I can bend to fasten my shoe laces without being out of breath. I would recommend it to anyone and I can't thank you enough.'

One lady who has arthritis in her knees and suffered from swelling feet said that she was 'able to walk better now with not so much pain – easier to go up stairs.' Another told me she had suffered for three years with a terrible pain in her back but since following the diet the pain had completely disappeared. As her weight loss was so gradual she couldn't believe that this was the cause so she attributed the benefit to the diet itself.

Before anyone commenced the diet I asked them to seek approval from their G.P. There was no doubt from the comments I received that their doctors were delighted with the format of the diet and were equally delighted with the results it achieved. Barbara Sewart, for instance, has angina and of course her doctor told her that this diet was particularly suitable for her. Since embarking on the diet Barbara has lost over a stone and her inch loss is quite remarkable. She comes along to my classes each week and it is wonderful to see how much more she can exercise now compared with when she first attended. She now participates in most of the exercises and her doctor can't believe the change and improvement in her

One volunteer was a diabetic. She reported that the diet was particularly suitable for her, just as it was for those with a high cholesterol level.

It was fun to read how many noticed an improvement in their temper as well as their waistline! Normally so many slimmers become irritable as they feel deprived and hungry. The majority on this diet, however, actually made a point of saying they never felt hungry, were able to eat similar foods to their family and never felt deprived. Many said they felt full after every meal and never needed to eat in between. In fact they positively loved the types of food included in the diet, particularly the freedom of choice, not having to count calories or units plus the fact that none of the food was expensive or difficult to purchase.

It was also surprising to hear that so many found it possible to stick to this diet when normally they found themselves lacking in the willpower department. As well as the generous amount of food they could consume, perhaps it was all that extra energy so many enjoyed instead of feeling drained and lethargic as with many diets.

I asked a variety of health-related questions within the questionnaire. I was particularly interested to hear if there had been any changes in the condition of skin, nails and hair. With so little fat in the diet I wouldn't have been surprised to receive reports of dryness, but I had no reason to worry.

Hair apparently benefitted: of the 120 volunteers a total of 37 stated that the condition of their hair had actually improved whilst almost all the remainder reported no deterioration whatsoever.

Skin benefited too. Here are some of the comments: 'My skin is more supple and not so dry.' 'My skin is a lot clearer.' 'My skin feels soft and healthy.' 'My skin is smoother and my hair more springy.' And I must add here that my own skin also became smoother and whilst at times I used to suffer from dry skin, strangely I no longer do.

The effect on volunteers' nails varied. Some reported incidence of splitting but many more reported that their nails had never been stronger and some said they now grew more quickly! In fact 31 stated the condition of their nails had definitely improved whilst the majority of the remainder reported no change in the condition.

I also enquired whether anyone had suffered from constipation whilst following the diet. Most who had previously suffered in this way reported a definite improvement and only a very few said they did suffer from constipation at first. With such a wide choice of foods I have no doubt that by selecting foods high in fibre in preference to others the condition would soon regulate itself. In general terms this diet is very high in fibre and should help everyone towards healthier bowels.

It was certainly good to read that so many people had never felt healthier or had more energy; and I was gratified to hear from those who had previously attempted to diet but without success that this diet had worked for them. We all know only too well how disheartening it can be to try hard but achieve nothing. The fact that my slimmers felt so much healthier encouraged them to continue on the diet while they were losing weight and it became clear that they had no intention of falling back in to their old habits. Following a low fat diet in the long term would certainly ensure that they did not regain all they had lost so far.

I smiled at how this lady summed up her experience of following the diet: 'I felt fine and was never hungry.

Now I can walk up hill without puffing and can bend down without grunting. I thank you.'

And last Christmas I received this letter from one of my Nottingham volunteers.

Dear Rosemary,

'I thought you would like to know that I'm still following your diet (almost anyway) and I have never felt better for years. I'm keeping at 11 stones and am fitter than I've ever been. I've done my own cleaning ready for Christmas which I hadn't the energy for in the spring and my husband and I walk about 3–4 miles every day. He has lost 1 stone and he is 73. We thank you for giving us the incentive to do this and wish you a Merry Christmas and happy New Year.

Yours sincerely,

K. Gill

P.S. I've just finished taking in all my skirts and trousers from 33 inch waist to 29 inch waist. I can't stop looking in the mirror.'

5
The diet

The following diet is based on the original Trial Diet but has now been amended taking into consideration the observations made by the trial team. For instance I have increased the skimmed milk allowance from 4 ounces to 10 ounces per day and I have allowed red meat to be included twice a week. This will make dining out much easier and of course extends the variety of protein foods beyond fish, chicken and cottage cheese!

The menu selections provide a basic guide but as you become more familiar with the fat content of all foods by studying the tables in Chapter 10 you will soon be able to formulate your own. I have given a list of strictly forbidden foods within this chapter to enable you to make a definite resolution, before you begin the diet, to ban them totally from your life! If you are going to cheat and sneak bars of chocolate or packets of salted peanuts into your cupboard to eat when no one's around then you might as well give this book to somebody else. This diet, if followed properly, will help you achieve the kind of figure you never dreamed possible but there is only one person in the world who can actually make it work for you – and that's YOU.

You will probably be very pleasantly surprised at the volume of food you are allowed and how you will feel really quite full after each meal. You will be delighted at how quickly you will begin to lose weight and inches and how different from previous diets this one proves to be. My volunteers really loved it and they couldn't believe they could actually lose weight yet eat so much. The additional energy they enjoyed after following the diet for a few weeks helped them to take on a much more positive attitude towards life – I could sense a really happy attitude in the remarks on the questionnaires.

The Diet

Eat three meals per day, selecting one meal from the Breakfast, Lunch and Dinner menus listed. And remember to restrict the consumption of red meat to just two helpings a week.

Daily allowance: 10 ounces (½ pint) skimmed low fat milk

Breakfasts

1. Porridge made with water, served with milk from allowance and two teaspoons of honey.
2. Five prunes plus a natural yogurt.
3. Fruit compote e.g. grapefruit, oranges, peaches, pineapple, pears, etc. (6 ounces total). Fruit may be tinned but must be in natural juice.
4. As much fresh fruit as you like, any type, but eaten at one sitting.
5. Tinned grapefruit in natural juice plus one slice wholemeal toast spread with one teaspoon of marmalade.
6. 8 oz can baked beans served on a slice of wholemeal toast.
7. 1 oz any cereal with a little sugar, moistened with fruit juice or skimmed milk from allowance.
8. 8 oz can tomatoes served on a slice of wholemeal toast.

Lunches – select one

1. Four to five pieces of any fresh fruit.
2. Jacket potato topped with 8 ounce can baked beans.
3. Jumbo sandwiches made with four slices of wholemeal bread thinly spread with Waistline or similar low calorie dressing, filled with salad – lettuce, cucumber, cress, tomatoes, sliced Spanish onion, beetroot, green and/or red peppers.
4. 2 slices of wholemeal toast with large (16 ounce) can of baked beans.
5. Rice salad: a bowl of chopped peppers, tomatoes, onion and cucumber mixed with cooked (boiled) brown rice and served with soy sauce.
6. Chicken joint (with skin removed) or prawns, served with a chopped salad of lettuce, cucumber, radish, spring onions, peppers, tomatoes, with soy sauce or yogurt dressing.
7. Jacket potato served with low fat cottage cheese and salad. (cottage cheese may be flavoured with chives, onions, pineapple, etc.).
8. Four Ryvitas or similar crispbread with 3 ounces chicken (no skin) or 1 ounce lean ham or lean roast beef (remove any fat), and Branston pickle plus two tomatoes and one piece of fresh fruit.
9. One carton low fat yogurt plus 8 ounces fresh fruit salad.
10. 4 ounces carton cottage cheese (with flavouring if preferred) with 4 Ryvitas or similar crispbread, plus salad.
11. Baked stuffed apple (one or two) filled with 1 ounce dried fruit, a few breadcrumbs and sweetened with honey or sweetener, served with plain low fat yogurt.
12. Clear or vegetable soup, served with one slice of toast and followed by two pieces of fresh fruit.

13. Jacket potato with 1 ounce roast beef, or roast pork or ham (with all fat removed) or 2 ounces chicken (no skin) served with Branston pickle and salad.
14. Two slices of wholemeal bread made into open sandwiches with prawns and salad, dressed with low-fat prawn cocktail dressing (see recipe).
15. Jacket potato served with sweetcorn and chopped salad.
16. Two slices wholemeal toast with small tin baked beans and small tin tomatoes.
17. 8 ounce carton low fat cottage cheese served with two tinned pear halves, chopped apple and celery, served on a bed of lettuce and garnished with tomato and cucumber.

Dinners – select one from each section, i.e. a starter, main course and dessert.

Starters

1. Wedge of melon.
2. Half a grapefruit.
3. Clear soup.
4. Melon balls in slimline ginger ale.
5. Grapefruit segments in natural juice.
6. Garlic mushrooms (see recipe).
7. Melon salad (see recipe).
8. French tomatoes (see recipe).

Main courses

1. 8 ounces steamed, grilled or microwaved white fish (cod, plaice, whiting, haddock, lemon sole, halibut) served with unlimited boiled vegetables.
2. 6 ounces chicken (no skin) steamed, grilled, baked or microwaved, and served with unlimited vegetables.
3. Chicken curry (see recipe) served with boiled brown rice.

4. Steamed or grilled or microwaved trout, stuffed with prawns and served with a large salad or assorted vegetables.

5. Barbecued chicken kebabs (see recipe) served with boiled brown rice.

6. Vegetable bake (see recipe).

7. 6 ounces calves' or lamb's liver, braised with onions, and served with unlimited vegetables.

8. Fish pie (see recipe) served with unlimited vegetables.

9. 4 ounces grilled rump steak with all fat removed, served with jacket potato and salad.

10. 3 ounces roast lamb with all fat removed, served with dry roast parsnips (see recipe) and unlimited vegetables.

11. 3 ounces roast leg of pork with all fat removed, served with apple sauce and unlimited vegetables.

12. 4 ounces roast duck (all skin removed) served with unlimited vegetables.

13. 6 ounces turkey (all skin removed) served with cranberry sauce, dry roast potatoes, and unlimited vegetables.

14. 3 ounces grilled or baked gammon steak or gammon rashers, with all fat removed, served with pineapple and unlimited vegetables.

15. 2 ounces bacon, grilled, with all fat removed, served with grilled tomatoes, baked beans and jacket or boiled potatoes.

16. 8-ounce chicken joint (weighed cooked including the bones), baked, with skin removed, in barbecue sauce (see recipe) and served with jacket potato or boiled brown rice and vegetables of your choice.

17. Prawn, chicken or vegetable chop suey (see recipes) served with boiled brown rice.

Desserts

1. Sliced banana topped with raspberry yogurt.
2. Fresh fruit salad topped with natural yogurt if desired.
3. Stuffed apple served with plain yogurt.
4. Strawberries served with strawberry yogurt.
5. Raspberries served with raspberry yogurt.
6. Pears cooked in red wine (see recipe).
7. Oranges in Cointreau (see recipe).
8. Pineapple in Kirsch (see recipe).
9. Sliced banana topped with fresh raspberries.
10. Fresh peaches sliced and served with fresh raspberries.
11. Any two pieces of fresh fruit.
12. Fruit sorbet – any flavour (see recipe).
13. Meringue basket filled with raspberries and topped with raspberry yogurt (or fill with strawberries or any fruit).
14. Pears in meringue (see recipe).

Drinks

Tea and coffee may be drunk freely if drunk black, or may be drunk white so long as skimmed milk allowance is not exceeded. Use artificial sweetener rather than sugar.

You may drink two alcoholic drinks per day. One drink means a single measure of spirit, a glass of wine, a small glass of sherry or half a pint of beer or lager. Slimline mixers should always be used and these may be drunk freely.

You may drink as much water as you like. Ashbourne or Perrier water taste wonderful.

Grape, apple, unsweetened orange, grapefruit, pineapple, or exotic fruit juices may be drunk in moderation. Some manufacturers are now producing juices with no artificial preservatives or added sugar – delicious and lower in calories too.

Daily nutritional requirements

Each day try to include at least the following:

6 ounces protein food (fish, poultry, meat, cottage cheese, baked beans).
12 ounces vegetables (including salad).
12 ounces fresh fruit
6 ounces carbohydrate (bread, cereals, potatoes, rice).
5 ounces low-fat yogurt
10 ounces skimmed milk

I would also suggest that one multivitamin tablet be taken daily to make doubly sure that you are getting all the vitamins you need.

The forbidden list

These foods are strictly forbidden whilst following the diet. Some will be reintroduced for the maintenance programme.

Butter, margarine, Flora, Gold, Outline, or any similar products
Cream, soured cream, whole milk, Gold Top, Silver Top, etc
Lard, oil (all kinds), dripping, suet, etc
Milk puddings of any kind
Fried foods of any kind
Fat or skin from all meats, poultry etc
All cheese except low fat cottage cheese
Egg yolk (the whites may be eaten freely)
Fatty fish including mackerel, kippers, roll mop herrings, eels, herrings, sardines, pilchards, bloater, salmon, sprats, tuna and whitebait
All nuts except chestnuts
Sunflower seeds
Goose
All fatty meats

Meat products, e.g. Scotch eggs, pork pie, faggots, black pudding, haggis, liver sausage, pâté

All types of sausages

All sauces containing cream or whole milk or eggs, e.g. salad dressing, mayonnaise, French dressing, parsley sauce, cheese sauce, Hollandaise sauce. (Waistline dressing may only be used as stated in the diet menus)

Cakes, sweet biscuits, pastries, sponge puddings, etc

Chocolate, toffees, fudge, caramel, butterscotch

Lemon curd

Marzipan

Cocoa and cocoa products, Horlicks

Crisps

Cream soups

Avocado pears

Yorkshire Pudding

Egg products, e.g. quiches, egg custard, pancakes etc.

6
Recipes

Garlic mushrooms
(Starter: serves 4)

1 lb button mushrooms
½ pint chicken stock
3 cloves fresh garlic
salt and pepper

Wash mushrooms and drain. Heat chicken stock with peeled and finely shredded garlic cloves. Boil for 5 minutes on gentle heat then add mushrooms and simmer in a covered saucepan for a further 7 minutes.

Because this dish is almost like a soup, with lots of stock, it is best served in soup dishes and eaten with a spoon.

Melon salad
(Starter: serves 4)

1 honeydew melon
1 lb tomatoes
1 large cucumber
salt
1 tablespoon parsley
1 heaped teaspoon mint and chives (chopped)
oil-free vinaigrette dressing (see recipe)

Cut the melon in half, remove the seeds and scoop out the flesh, ideally with a curved grapefruit knife. Cut the flesh into cubes.

Skin and quarter the tomatoes, squeeze out the seeds and remove the core; cut into quarters again if the tomatoes are large.

Peel the cucumber, cut into small cubes of similar size to the melon cubes. Sprinkle with salt, cover with a plate and stand for 30 minutes. Drain away any liquid and rinse cubes in cold water.

Mix the fruit and vegetables together in a deep bowl; pour over the dressing; cover and chill for 2–3 hours. Just before serving, mix in the herbs.

As the salad makes a lot of juice it should be eaten with a spoon. A herb loaf (see recipe) goes well with melon salad.

French Tomatoes

(Starter: serves 4)

French Tomatoes are so called because in the traditional recipe French cream cheese is used in place of the low fat cottage cheese.

8 tomatoes
salt and pepper
6 oz Shape low fat cottage cheese
small bunch of fresh chives,
or chopped spring onion tops or parsley
watercress to garnish
oil-free vinaigrette dressing (see recipe)

Method
Scald and skin the tomatoes by placing them in a bowl, pouring boiling water over them, counting to fifteen before pouring off the hot water and replacing it with cold. The skin then comes off easily. Cut a slice from the non-stalk end of each tomato and reserve slices. Hold tomato in the palm of your hand and remove seeds with the handle of a teaspoon, then remove the core with the

bowl of the spoon. Drain the hollowed-out tomato and season lightly inside each one with salt.

Soften cheese with a fork and add finely chopped chives, parsley or spring onion tops and season well. Fill the tomatoes with the cheese mixture, using a small teaspoon, until the mixture is above the rim of the tomato. Replace their top slices on the slant and arrange them in a serving dish.

Make dressing (see recipe) and spoon over the tomatoes, reserving a couple of spoonfuls until just before serving. Chill filled tomatoes for up to two hours. Garnish with watercress and sprinkle remaining chives over tomatoes.

Stilton Pears

(Starter: Maintenance programme; serves 4)

6 ripe pears
(or 12 tinned pear halves if fresh not available)
2 oz Stilton cheese
8 oz Shape soft low fat cheese
2 tablespoons skimmed milk
salt and pepper
juice of 1 lemon
1 oz flaked almonds, baked until brown

Peel pears and cut in half lengthways. Remove core with the bowl of a spoon and paint lemon juice all over pears to prevent discolouration. Crush Stilton with a fork and work until creamy, then mix with the Shape soft cheese and skimmed milk until smooth. Season to taste. With a teaspoon, pile cheese mixture into cavities left by the removal of the cores in the pear halves. Sprinkle browned flaked almonds on top and serve on a bed of lettuce.

Chicken curry

(Main course: serves 2)

2 chicken joints with all fat and skin removed
16 oz tin tomatoes
bay leaf
1 eating apple, cored and chopped small
2 teaspoons Branston pickle
1 teaspoon tomato purée
1 medium onion, finely chopped
1 tablespoon curry powder

Place the chicken joints and all the other ingredients in a saucepan and bring to the boil. Put a lid on the saucepan and cook slowly for about one hour, stirring occasionally and making sure the chicken joints are turned every fifteen minutes or so. If the mixture is too thin, remove the lid and cook on a slightly higher heat until the sauce reduces and thickens.

Serve on a bed of boiled rice, preferably brown rice.

Barbecued Chicken Kebabs

(Main course: serves 2)

For kebabs:
2 large chicken joints, preferably breasts, boned and
with all fat and skin removed
2 medium sized onions peeled and cut into quarters
1 green pepper with core and seeds removed, cut into
bite-sized squares
1 red pepper
6 oz mushrooms, washed but left whole
8 bay leaves

For barbecue sauce:
2 tablespoons tomato ketchup
2 tablespoons brown sauce
2 tablespoons mushroom sauce (optional)
2 tablespoons wine vinegar

Cut the chicken flesh into cubes about ½–¾ inch square. Place on to skewers alternately with pieces of onion, green and red peppers and the mushrooms, adding a bay leaf to the skewers at intervals to give flavour.

Mix all the sauce ingredients together and brush on to the skewers filled with the chicken and vegetables. If possible, brush the sauce on a couple of hours before cooking as this will add greatly to the flavour. Keep any remaining sauce ready for basting.

Place the skewers under the grill and cook under a moderate heat turning frequently to avoid burning. Baste frequently with the sauce mixture to maintain the moisture. Use no fat.

Serve on a bed of boiled rice (preferable brown rice) and grilled fresh tomatoes.

Vegetable Bake

(Main course: serves 1)

Selection of any vegetables, e.g. carrots, parsnips,
potatoes, peas, cabbage, leeks, onions
4 oz mushrooms, washed
cup of breadcrumbs – preferably wholemeal
½ pint vegetable stock
1 teaspoon mixed herbs

Partly cook the vegetables, chop them up and place in layers in a large ovenproof dish. Sprinkle the mixed herbs between each layer and finally slice the mushrooms and place over the top of the vegetables. Sprinkle with the breadcrumbs and then moisten the contents of the dish with the vegetable stock. Bake in a moderate oven (180°, 350° F, Gas Mark 4) for 20 minutes until piping hot.

Fish Pie

(Main course: serves 4)

1½ lbs cod
1½ lbs potatoes
Salt and pepper
For those on the maintenance programme only: 2 oz
Shape or Tendale 'Cheddar' if desired

Bake, steam or microwave the fish but do not overcook.
Season well.

Boil the potatoes until well done and mash with a
little water to achieve a soft consistency. Season well.

Place fish in an ovenproof dish. Flake the flesh, remove
the skin and evenly distribute the fish across the base of
the dish. Sprinkle the grated cheese at this point if
desired. Cover the fish completely with the mashed
potatoes and smooth over with a fork. Sprinkle a little
cheese on the top if desired. If the ingredients are still
hot just place under a hot grill for a few minutes to
brown the top. Alternatively the pie can be made well
in advance and then warmed through in a moderate
oven for 20 minutes, or microwaved on high for 5
minutes.

Vegetable Chop Suey

(Main course: serves 2)

1 large onion, finely sliced
1 sweet pepper (green or red)
with core and seeds removed
and flesh finely shredded
2 large carrots, peeled and coarsely grated
3 sticks celery, finely sliced
1 can (8 oz) bean sprouts

Heat a large non-stick or stainless steel frying pan (or wok) and add the onion, pepper, carrots and celery. Shake the pan over moderate heat until the vegetables are barely cooked, then add the drained bean sprouts and fork them together well. Keep moving the contents of the pan to avoid burning.

Prawns or sliced chicken can also be added with the bean sprouts if desired.

Serve hot with soy sauce.

Baked (Jacket) Potatoes

1 large potato per person
salt

Scrub the potatoes well and make a single cut along the top of each. Roll them in salt and bake for one and a half hours (or until they 'give' when pressed) in a moderately hot oven (190°, 375°F, Gas Mark 5). Make cross-cuts on top of each potato and squeeze to enlarge cuts. Add filling of your choice. Serve at once.

Alternative serving suggestion
(*Maintenance programme: serves 4*)
Remove potato centres and place in a bowl, carefully preserving 'jackets'. Add one chopped onion, 2 oz Shape or Tendale cheddar flavour cheese, coarsely grated, salt and black pepper. Mix thoroughly and replace in potato skins. Return to the oven for ten minutes to heat through before serving.

Dry Roast Potatoes

Choose medium to large potatoes of even size.

Peel and blanch by putting into cold salted water and bringing to the boil.

Drain thoroughly, lightly scratch the surface with a fork and sprinkle lightly with salt. Place in a non-stick baking tray, without fat, in a hot oven for about 1–1½ hours.

Dry Roast Parsnips

Choose evenly sized medium parsnips.

Peel and blanch halved parsnips in cold salted water and bring to the boil. Drain thoroughly and sprinkle lightly with salt. Place in a non-stick baking tray, without fat, in a moderate oven for 30 minutes. Cook until soft in the centre when pierced with a fork.

Stuffed Mushrooms
(*Starter*)

2 large mushrooms per person, and two or three over
2 oz stock (vegetable or chicken)
1 teaspoon chopped onion
1 tablespoon fresh white breadcrumbs
Salt and pepper
1 teaspon parsley
pinch of dried mixed herbs

Cup mushrooms are best for this dish. Wash and peel 2 mushrooms per person and cut the stalks across level with the caps (this helps prevent shrinkage).

Chop the trimmings along with the rest of the mushrooms. Cook the chopped mushrooms for 1–2 minutes in the stock with the chopped onion. Add the crumbs, season and add herbs.

Spread this mixture on to the whole mushrooms and arrange them on a baking sheet or in a fireproof dish. Bake for 12–15 minutes in a moderately hot oven (190°C, 375°F, Gas Mark 5). Serve immediately.

Pears in Red Wine

(Dessert: Serves 4)

6 ripe pears, peeled but left whole
2 oz brown sugar
10 fl oz red wine
2 fl oz water
½ level teaspoon cinnamon or ground ginger

Combine wine, water, sugar and spice in a glass jug and microwave on high for approximately 4 minutes or until boiling, or boil in a saucepan.
Either: place the pears in the saucepan with the boiled wine mixture and simmer for 10–15 minutes, turning the pears carefully from time to time to ensure even colouring.
Or: (for microwaving) place the pears in a deep dish, e.g. soufflé type, pour wine sauce over them and cover with cling film. Microwave on *high* for approximately 5 minutes or until just tender but retaining their shape.

Serve hot or cold (with Shape Single or ice cream if desired by those on maintenance programme only).

Oranges in Cointreau

(Dessert: serves 4)

6 oranges – medium size
wine glass of medium to sweet white wine, *or* fresh orange juice
sherry glass of Cointreau or Grand Marnier liqueur
artificial sweetener if desired

Heat white wine or orange juice and liqueur in a saucepan and add sweetener to taste. Allow to cool.

Carefully peel the oranges with a sharp knife to remove all pith. This can be done by slicing off the peel across the top of the orange and using this flat end of the orange as a base. Cut strips of peel away from the top downwards with a very sharp knife so that the orange is completely free from the white membranes of the peel. Squeeze the peel to extract any juice and pour this into the wine mixture.

Slice the orange across to form round slices of equal size. Place in the cooled liquid and allow to stand in a refrigerator for at least 12 hours.

Serve in glass dishes

Pineapple in Kirsch

(Dessert: Serves 4)

1 fresh pineapple
3 fluid oz Kirsch

Remove skin and core from the pineapple and slice into rings.

Sprinkle the Kirsch over the fruit and place in a refrigerator for at least 12 hours to marinate. Keep turning the fruit to ensure even flavouring.

Serve with Shape Single or ice cream if desired by those on maintenance programme only.

Fruit Sorbet

(Dessert: serves 6)

1lb fruit making:
¼ pint fruit purée
(preferably a strong-flavoured fruit
e.g. blackcurrant, blackberry, strawberry,
raspberry or black cherries. Canned fruit
may be used but remove syrup
before liquidizing)
2 large egg whites
Artificial sweetener to taste (if desired)

If fresh fruit is used cook approximately 1 lb of fruit in very little water together with a sweetening agent if desired. When the fruit is soft and the liquid well coloured *either* place the cooked fruit in a sieve and work the pulp with a wooden spoon until as much as possible of the fruit has passed through the mesh *or* use a liquidizer. Allow to cool and place the purée in a plastic container; cover with a lid and freeze until it begins to set. When a layer of purée approximately ½ inch thick has frozen, remove the mixture from the freezer and stir it so that the mixture is a soft crystallized consistency.

Whisk the two egg whites until stiff and standing in peaks. Fold into the semi-frozen purée to give a marbled effect. Immediately refreeze the mixture and freeze until firm. Serve straight from the freezer.

Pears in Meringue

(Dessert: serves 4)

6 ripe dessert pears, peeled but left whole
10 fl oz apple juice
3 egg whites
6 oz caster sugar

71

Cook the pears in the apple juice until just tender but still firm. Cut a slice off the bottom of each pear to enable them to sit in a dish without falling over, and place in an ovenproof dish well spaced out.

Whisk the egg whites in a large and completely grease-free bowl, preferably with a balloon whisk or rotary beater. (Do not use an electric whisk as this is too strong and it will over-beat the egg whites.)

When the whites are firm and stand in peaks, whisk in 1 tablespoon of the caster sugar for 1 minute. Fold in the remainder of the sugar with a metal spoon, cutting the egg whites rather than mixing them.

Place the egg white and sugar mixture into a large piping bag with a metal nozzle (any pattern) and pipe a pyramid around each pear starting from the base and working upwards. Place in a warm oven (160°C, 325°F, Gas Mark 3) and cook until firm and golden.

Serve hot or cold (with Shape Single or ice cream if desired by those on maintenance programme only).

Apple Gâteau

(Maintenance programme: Makes one 20 cm/8 inch cake, serving 8)

3 eggs
4½ oz caster sugar
3 oz plain flour
pinch of salt
1 lb eating apples, peeled, cored and sliced
grated rind and juice of 1 lemon
1 tablespoon apricot jam
artificial sweetener for apples if desired
1 teaspoon icing sugar

Very lightly grease 8 inch cake tin; dust with caster sugar and then with flour. Shake out the excess.

Place the eggs and caster sugar in a mixing bowl and

whisk with an electric whisk/mixer for 5 minutes at top speed. When thick and mousse-like, fold in the sifted flour and salt. Pour into the prepared tin. Bake in the centre of a moderately hot oven (190°C, 375°F., Gas Mark 5) for 25 minutes or until golden brown and shrunk from the edges of the tin a little. Run a blunt knife around the inside edge of the tin and turn out the cake on to a wire rack to cool.

For the filling, place the apple slices in a pan with the grated rind and juice of a lemon and the jam. Heat slowly. Add the artificial sweetener to taste if required. Cover and cook until the apples are just tender. When the cake is cool, slice it across with a large knife to make two cakes. Spread the bottom half with the cooled apple filling and cover with the top half of the cake. Sprinkle with icing sugar on top.

Hot Herb Loaf
(Maintenance Programme)

1 French loaf
4 oz St Ivel Gold or similar low fat spread
1 tablespoon mixed dried herbs
juice of ¼ lemon
black pepper
2 cloves of fresh garlic, crushed

Cream the low fat spread with the herbs, lemon juice and seasoning. If you like garlic, add a little now.

Cut the loaf into even slanting slices about 1 inch thick. Spread each slice generously with low-fat spread mixture and reshape loaf. Wrap in foil and bake for 10 minutes in a hot oven at 220°C, 425°F, Gas Mark 7. Then reduce oven setting to 200°C, 400°F, Gas Mark 6 and open the foil so that the bread browns and crisps. This should take a further 5–8 minutes.

(For those wishing to avoid the use of any fat, leave some slices without the spread, sprinkling them with herbs, lemon juice and garlic only).

Barbecue Sauce

1 teaspoon plain flour
1/3 pint potato stock
1 tablespoon soy sauce
dash Worcester sauce
salt and pepper
small tin tomatoes

Skim off all fat from grill pan after cooking meat or poultry, leaving any sediment. Stir in the flour, add a tablespoon of the stock and cook very gently for 2–3 minutes. Remove from the heat, and blend in potato stock, sauces and seasoning. Return to heat and stir until boiling. Add the tinned tomatoes finely chopped (scissor snipped). Simmer for a minute or until the sauce has a creamy consistency.

This sauce goes well with kebabs and with grilled or baked chicken.

Prawn Cocktail Dressing
Serves 2

2 tablespoons tomato ketchup
1 tablespoon low calorie salad dressing (e.g. Waistline, Heinz Weight Watchers' Dressing)
squeeze of lemon juice

Mix all ingredients together and add to prawns.

Oil-free Vinaigrette Dressing

3 tablespoons white wine vinegar or cider vinegar
1 tablespoon lemon juice
½ teaspoon black pepper
½ teaspoon salt
1 teaspoon sugar
Chopped herbs (thyme, marjoram, basil or parsley)

Mix all the ingredients together. Place in a sealed container and shake well. Taste and add more salt or sugar as desired.

Drinks

Grapefruit Fizz
unsweetened grapefruit juice
slimline tonic water

Pour approximately 4 fl oz unsweetened grapefruit juice into a tall glass and add plenty of ice. Top up with the slimline tonic.

This drink is an excellent 'filler' before a meal.

St Clements
Slimline Orange
Slimline Bitter Lemon

Pour equal quantities of each into a tall glass filled with ice. Top up as required.

For an extra special drink use freshly squeezed orange juice with the bitter lemon.

4
Spritzer
5 fl oz white wine
Sparkling mineral water

Pour the wine into a large wineglass and add the mineral water. This provides a long and very enjoyable drink that can accompany a meal, or just be drunk for pleasure socially.

7
What is cellulite?

Cellulite is the particularly ugly type of fat found around the hips, thighs and upper arms. The texture of the skin is quite different from the skin elsewhere on our body; it appears puckered, dimpled and can resemble orange peel when it is pinched. If you sit on a chair next to a mirror, without the cosmetic benefits of tights of course, you will see the skin texture clearly. A friend of mine realized how much cellulite she had when her little girl spotted her sitting on the loo, bare flesh displayed. 'Why have you got holes in your leg, Mummy?' she enquired and that, I am afraid to say, is what cellulite looks like. An ugly area of fat which is very uneven and very unattractive.

In more technical terms cellulite is a modified form of fat tissue to be found just below the surface of the skin. It all begins with the stagnation of the blood in capillaries (tiny blood vessels), and this leads to a flow of blood fluids (plasma) through the capillary walls which separate fat-storing cells known as adipose cells. Small groups of these cells become surrounded by collagen fibre bundles in what are known as micronodules. These in turn group together to form macronodules which are responsible for the skin's irregular, wrinkled appearance. It is this uneven appearance that distinguishes cellulite from neighbouring fat on the tummy or waist which is almost always relatively smooth and uniform.

Our bodies use these fat cells and the connective tissue as a kind of storehouse for waste products and because these particular fat cells are metabolically less active than other cells in the body they make an ideal location for whatever toxic waste products the body would like to keep out of the way so that they don't pollute the bloodstream. It is easy to see, therefore, that the problem is a particularly difficult one to solve as the area is partially 'cut off' from our normal circulation.

Consequently these areas are the first to exhibit extra fat and the last to actually reduce. In fact it is not only the overweight who suffer from cellulite, it can also be witnessed on thin women.

Men do not suffer with cellulite even when obese. It is a problem only afflicting women and only after puberty, so it is easy to see that the condition is connected with our hormones. Clinical investigations produced evidence that 75% of the women questioned who developed cellulite, did so at a time of hormonal change. In fact 12% developed it at puberty, 17% during pregnancy, 19% when they started taking the birth pill and 27% at the onset of the menopause. The link between the female hormones and predisposition to cellulite becomes even clearer when you consider that oestrogen is also instrumental in controlling fluid retention and this in itself is the crux of the cellulite problem. The female hormonal cycle is finely synchronized with the circulatory system and lymphatic drainage in particular. Faulty circulation is thought to be the root cause of the disorder.

Stress and our inability to cope with it can be an important cellulite trigger because it affects the hypothalamus 'master gland' which controls all other hormonal functions.

Dietary factors also have a very important part to play as a diet high in junk food encourages the deposit of fat, particularly in the 'waste ground' around our hips, thighs and arms. Foods such as sugar, salt, spices, fat and alcohol can therefore aggravate a cellulite condition by cluttering up the system with additional waste matter that is poorly eliminated. Constipation can also encourage cellulite formation – if the waste matter is not leaving the body through the normal channels the body will store it away from the bloodstream and again the islands of fat cells causing cellulite provide the perfect storehouse.

Our lifestyle should also be taken into consideration. A sedentary existence or a job that keeps you standing around for hours is liable to encourage a poor circulation as well as allowing the buttock and thigh muscles to become weak and flabby, making cellulite much worse. For similar reasons bad posture can be to blame for congestion and erratic circulation in the lower part of the body.

There is also the hereditary factor and cellulite does tend to run in families, so you may have your mother to thank for passing it on to you! Obviously we cannot choose our parents but we can do a great deal to improve the shape, form and texture of these problem areas. This can be done in three forms – diet, exercise and treatment of the surface of the skin. A combination of all three would certainly be the ideal.

Diet
A diet high in fresh fruit and vegetables is obviously to be recommended as it encourages digestion and elimination. These are also very healthy foods rich in vitamins and minerals. Wholegrain cereals are also good for the same reasons, and protein foods (meat, fish, eggs and cheese) taken in moderation help to balance the diet and give all the necessary nutrients. Skimmed milk and low fat spreads should also be preferred to the full fat equivalents in the family diet. Foods high in sugar, salt, fat and spices should be kept to a minimum, and the consumption of alcohol should be restricted too.

Exercise
Slow, rhythmic or stretching exercises should be undertaken in preference to jogging and jumping-about type exercises. A stretching type of exercise will

encourage muscle tone without jolting the fat cells and therefore encouraging the development of the clusters of sedentary fat cells which form cellulite.

Surface treatment
As cellulite is caused by poor circulation any massage or activity to stimulate the circulation will certainly help to improve the texture and the appearance of the affected areas. Massage gloves and creams designed to help the particular problem will help improve the contours of the body.

Ever since I reached my teens I have suffered with cellulite. My mother also had it and when I had previously attempted to diet and had successfully lost weight there was little improvement, if any, to the appearance of my ugly dimpled thighs, that is until I went on my low fat diet. I just couldn't believe the remarkable improvement. My thighs were far from being perfect but, my goodness, they did look much better. After a while I thought I would help them along with some cellulite massage cream. I used Vichy's Hip and Thigh Massage Cream and I could actually feel the nodules of fat cells disintegrating after a few weeks of applying the cream daily, and the improvement became more and more obvious as I continued.

Just as I was fascinated with the reduction in inches from my own thighs when I first embarked on my special diet, I was equally interested to hear whether my trial team had benefited in the cellulite department and I included a question to this effect in my questionnaire. Forty-three out of the 123 reported a definite reduction in cellulite and a further 35 said they thought it *had* improved. This meant that 78 had witnessed a benefit. Only 13 said they saw no improvement; 27 weren't sure but didn't think there was any change; and the remaining 5 didn't answer the question.

So here we see again that whilst most diets are ineffective in reducing inches and cellulite, my new diet again came up trumps. The evidence in terms of inch loss recorded by my trial team proves without doubt that the reduction of fat and the increase in fresh fruit and vegetables in our diet really does reduce cellulite, despite all the hormonal, stress, lifestyle and postural factors which could have caused it. I am not saying that the diet will completely eliminate cellulite but I do believe it will significantly reduce it. Of course the foods suggested within the diet are very wholesome with very little junk food. Many of my volunteers commented on how much they enjoyed eating so much fruit and vegetables and how much fitter they felt, so I have no doubt that it is the reduction of fat and the increase in better, healthier food that together helped produce such positive benefits.

There are, of course, other ways cellulite can be reduced, for instance by Mesotherapy which is the multi-injection of substances such as hormones, local anaesthetics, thyroxine, theophylline, lipolytic agents, Centella asiatica, aminophylline, mild diuretics, hyalase, mucopolysaccharides, and B vitamins. There are also a wide variety of more drastic therapies ranging from laser beam therapy to selective lipectomy which is the insertion of a hypotonic solution into the problem areas and suction of lipolysed fat. I have seen some of these treatments carried out on patients and it looks horrific. I've heard also of courses of injections which remove it in the short term but result in a worse incidence of cellulite after the treatment has worn off. All of these methods are extremely costly and frankly are not helping the initial *cause* of the problem.

Topical creams, such as the hip and thigh cream which I used, are usually based upon plant extracts which affect the circulation just below the skin. The choice of cream base is very important in maintaining the stability of the active substance and in controlling its absorption by the skin. The ease of application, fluidity and prompt absorption are of prime importance for such products and the massaging action on the affected area helps to activate the ingredients of the cream and improve circulation. The cream need only be lightly massaged with the finger tips either once or twice a day and the manufacturers stress that you do not have to knead or use a special applicator. After two weeks of regular use an improvement should be visible, with a further improvement if the applications are continued for four weeks.

Vichy conducted their own test on 47 women. Thirty-one showed positive results after four weeks and everyone reported that their skin felt smoother, more supple and better toned.

One of the latest surface treatments has been produced by Biotherm. It is called the Ten Day Thermo Active Body Contouring Treatment and it contains methyl nicotinate. This gives a warming effect to stimulate the microcirculation and aids penetration of the other active ingredients. The treatment is quite expensive but produces visible benefits after just ten days. It brings about a shrinkage of the cellulite areas, recontours the silhouette, and improves the skin's elasticity. If it is as effective as the researchers say it is I am sure it is going to be a very big hit with cellulite sufferers world-wide.

If you have a really bad cellulite problem I suggest you follow the diet and try and take some sensible form of daily exercise even if it is only walking the dog for a couple of miles. A treatment cream will then help you to improve the condition to an acceptable level and I would certainly try all of these methods conscientiously before even considering the much more serious courses of action – injections or surgery.

8
Exercises – Do they help or hinder?

Regular moderate exercise offers three main benefits. Firstly it is good for our health since it strengthens the heart, secondly it burns up extra calories and helps to increase our metabolic rate, and thirdly it improves the contours of our body. As we all know, a well-toned body is a delight to be seen. The fact that regular exercise is beneficial is therefore beyond question. Only those with a medical problem which might be aggravated by physical activity should hesitate before stepping into action, but providing they have a word with their doctor first, even severely disabled people will usually benefit from some kind of exercise.

Exercise is a word which covers a vast array of activities. It could mean being energetic, as in running a marathon, or tranquil, as in practising yoga. Whatever the activity, most forms of exercise are good for us, but often the benefits are as varied as the activities themselves. True physical fitness is something more than being able to cope with the stresses and strains of everyday life. It consists of three important ingredients – *stamina, suppleness* and *strength*. Whilst running a marathon requires a great deal of stamina, yoga is undoubtedly the best way to improve suppleness while weight-lifting obviously develops strength. Swimming incorporates all three aspects, and a good squash player depends more on suppleness and stamina. So let's look more closely at these three 'S' factors, as they are often called.

Perhaps the most important is *stamina* as this provides the staying power and the ability to keep on going without feeling you're going to collapse. For stamina we need a good circulation in the heart muscle and the other muscles of the body to ensure that oxygen reaches the parts that particularly need it. A person who has plenty of stamina will have a slower and more powerful heartbeat and they will cope more easily with prolonged or heavy exertion.

Suppleness or flexibility gives you a greater range of movements which will help you avoid the problems of pulled muscles and tendons and sprained ligaments. The greater your mobility the less likely you will be to suffer aches and pains brought on by stiffness. Suppleness helps to keep you looking younger too as you will be able to move and walk better in later years.

The development of *strength* can prevent a multitude of problems occurring throughout our lives. We all find ourselves in a situation at some time where we have to carry a very heavy suitcase, or where a parcel has been delivered and has to be lifted into the house. All kinds of little situations like this can cause enormous problems, so having a bit of extra muscle-power will insure us against possible injury.

Your choice of exercise must also depend on your general state of health. It is stupid to rush into the sort of vigorous exercise that may aggravate a medical condition and, of course, it also depends on how fit you are already.

Always wear the right clothing for the activity you choose – clothing worn too tight can hinder circulation. Be sure to wear the correct footwear to prevent injuries to your feet, legs and back, not only because they can be acutely painful but because such injuries can take months to mend.

Perhaps the most important thing to remember about exercise is that it *must* be enjoyable. If it isn't, you are unlikely to continue. Exercise isn't a craze we take up seriously one day and dismiss as 'not for me' two weeks later because we've overdone it. No one will benefit from such a short spell. Rather like good eating habits, the rewards are reaped weeks, if not months or even years later.

If you want to tone up your body and develop a better shape there is no doubt that swimming, keep-fit exercises and yoga will help enormously. You can expect to see a visible improvement within a few months of regular practice. If it's stamina and feeling 'fitter' that you want then probably a sport such as badminton, squash or tennis will do the trick. Strength can be developed by digging the garden, weight-lifting, rowing or swimming hard. In fact swimming is undoubtedly the best possible form of exercise – not only because it develops stamina, suppleness *and* strength but because the buoyancy of the water removes the danger of straining an otherwise unfit body. Your stamina will dictate your endurance and you will soon be able to measure your improved fitness by seeing how much further you can swim.

Certain exercises can have the effect of developing muscles to an excessive degree – for instance cycling, whilst good for the thighs and hips, will possibly over-develop the calf muscles. Running or jumping exercises can encourage cellulite and swimming will develop the muscles in the shoulders. Obviously weight-lifting will develop many muscles.

However we are unlikely to develop a great deal of extra muscle by normal sporting activities; we are much more likely to improve muscle tone.

Before you undertake any form of exercise it is very important that you warm up properly. Failure to do so is likely to cause injury. Circulation of blood around the body is comparatively slow when we are just going about our normal daily tasks. Our pulse rate tells us how slowly if we count the beats. A normal resting heartbeat is around 70–80 beats a minute. But when we exercise we need more oxygen and we can only get that by pumping more blood around our body. This increased blood flow then increases the circulation into our muscles and the body becomes warm and ready for action. If we don't warm up first we can easily pull a muscle or tear a ligament, just as the elasticity in a rubber band is greater if it is warm than if it is cold.

A walking jog on the spot combined with various gentle stretching movements will help to build up the heartbeat and improve the circulation of blood throughout the body. You can, if you wish, test your heartbeat by taking your pulse for ten seconds and multiplying it by six thus making a minute. You are sufficiently warmed up when your pulse rate is significantly faster than when taken at rest. It is easy to calculate your personal *maximum* heartrate by deducting your age from 220, and you are sufficiently warmed up when your heartrate is between 60% and 90% of your maximum. Skipping with a rope for a few minutes is also a good way to warm up. Alternatively, a few exercises suitable for the warm up are shown over the page.

The warm up

These exercises are for a general all over warm-up. Practise to bouncy music and repeat each exercise at least ten times.

Jogging

Jogging side to side

Jog with heels high

Scissor jumps backward and forward

Bounce the knees

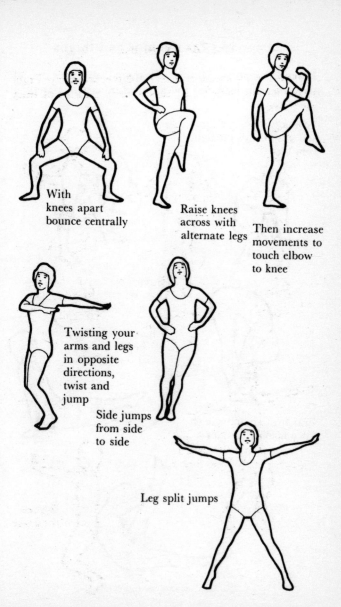

With knees apart bounce centrally

Raise knees across with alternate legs

Then increase movements to touch elbow to knee

Twisting your arms and legs in opposite directions, twist and jump

Side jumps from side to side

Leg split jumps

Exercises for the hips and thighs

Practise to music with a 4/4 tempo and repeat each movement at least ten times unless otherwise stated.

Bend forward
and push hands through
your legs

Stretch over to one leg twice
then repeat with other leg

Bounce legs out and in
5 steps each way
and repeat 5 times

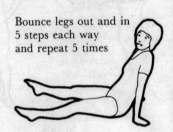

Straighten up and stretch
down holding both legs

Raise alternate straight legs

With legs apart, raise arms and stretch back

Then reach down and bounce your head toward your knee. Alternate sides each time

Sit up, stretch forward, relax head to knees

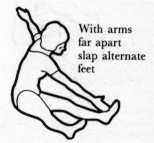

With arms far apart slap alternate feet

Place one hand on your heel and lean back and stretch. Repeat to each side

Leg stretch   Bounce and   Bounce with leg extended.
straighten   Change sides

Advanced side bend with leg extended 4 to each side.
Repeat 3 times

Cancan steps
with legs straight

Thrust your legs out and bounce

Crouch and bounce

Leg raises

and together

Knee bends and stretch

Roll over after completing these movements on one side and perform the same movements again

Kneeling on the floor raise leg up . . . and down

Using your arms and hands to
support you, raise your hips
and then squeeze knee muscles
without altering the position of
your legs

Raise bent leg sideways

Place weight forward and lower
hips. Curl spine and keep head up

Then raise feet
behind you

Repeat each exercise 10 times and practise to fast-tempo
music

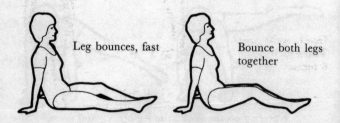

Leg bounces, fast

Bounce both legs
together

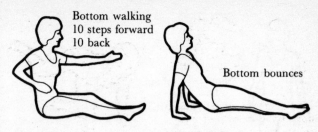

Bottom walking
10 steps forward
10 back

Bottom bounces

The warm down

Just as it is essential to warm up when you begin your exercise session it is also important to warm down after every session to help your heart beat return to normal.

Repeat these warm down exercises as directed:

Gentle side bends.
Each side 6 times

Gentle waist twists.
Twice each side,
6 times

Head rolls.
Each side 5 times

Shoulder circling,
10 backward
and 10 forward

Slowly lie down and relax
completely for 5 minutes

In order to become fitter, develop muscle tone and flexibility, we must exercise ideally three times a week. Each session can be different, for example a game of squash or badminton on Monday, keep fit class on Wednesday and a good walk on Saturday. The secret is to keep it varied, keep it interesting and *enjoy* it. And if you practise at least some of the exercises described in this book every day, you will soon see a change in your hips and thighs.

9
Slim thighs for ever

Losing weight by following any reducing diet is comparatively easy but usually the problems arise once you stop.

Following any new pattern of eating and seeing the pounds and inches disappearing in front of your very eyes can be very rewarding and even fun but slimmers are often disillusioned once they cease dieting, return to normal eating and the pounds pile back on – it all seems so unfair!

After you have followed *this* diet for a minimum of eight weeks, not only will you have enjoyed enormous benefits in the re-forming of your body shape but I have no doubt that you will *feel* significantly healthier too. During the period of actually trying to reduce your weight and inches you have been consuming *fewer* calories than your body has been using and therefore your excess stores of fat have been reduced. After you have reached your ideal weight, or shape, you will have to *increase* the number of calories so that you don't continue to slim. There is no point in becoming too slim – it is both unattractive and unhealthy so we must know when to stop. Conversely, it is very important that you do not return to all the old eating habits that made you overweight in the first place – so this chapter is perhaps the most important in the book. It is going to show you how to *stay* the new *slim shape* that you are now, or will be after following the diet.

Let me first explain how diets work. We burn up energy in being alive and going about our daily tasks, rather like a car burns petrol when it goes on a journey.

But unlike a car, we carry on burning fuel when we go to bed or just sit down – because we need energy to keep the heart pumping, lungs breathing, hair growing, tissues renewing, etc. The more active we are the more energy, or calories, we use. When we lose weight we are taking in fewer calories than we use so the body draws on its reserve stores, but after a while our body regulates to the lower calorie intake and begins to need less and less – and that's why we find it difficult to lose weight when we have been on a diet for a long time. The amount of energy we need is measured by the basal metabolic rate and it is this metabolic rate that slows down after a reduction in calories has been taken over a period of time. This means that, unfortunately, we cannot stop dieting one day having reached our goal and then return to normal eating straight away, as what was 'normal eating' three months ago is now considered by the body to be 'overeating' and we would find that we gained weight very easily indeed. All very unfair and frustrating, I know, but we can overcome the problem with a little thought and patience. If the metabolic rate can be reduced it can also be increased providing it is done slowly and carefully. This is how it can be done.

As we learned in the cellulite chapter, junk food is often stored and distributed more easily than good wholesome healthy food which is utilized by our body. So avoid less nutritious foods particularly after you have reached your goal weight. However, we can increase the amount of 'good' food and that can mean introducing a little more protein food – more meat, a few eggs, a little cheese, and more poultry or fish as desired. You can also slowly include a little fat – not whole fat like butter or margarine but the low fat spreads like Gold or Outline.

You can even have the occasional serving of chips. 'Marvellous' I hear you say! You can have some ordinary cheese grated on to your jacket potato but don't think that you can have loads of these wonderful things all in the same week and not gain weight! You must take it carefully and if you allow yourself a helping of chips one day, don't have anything else that would be considered high in fat for the rest of that day.

Fat is the highest calorific food there is and by cutting it down we are helping to keep our calories down to a reasonable level. No one enjoys calorie counting and I do not recommend that you start it now on this maintenance programme but we must realize that if you start consuming vast quantities of all the foods that you have either considerably reduced in your diet or even eliminated, you will inevitably undo all the good that you have achieved.

Some of my trial team wrote to me saying that if they did regain a few pounds they found it easy to revert to the diet for a week or so and the pounds were easily lost again but as many a yo-yo dieter will know, the more times you do this the more difficult it is to achieve the same success. So I recommend prevention rather than cure, and the following recommendations will help you maintain your success.

The following lists of foods and recommendations should form the pattern of foods consumed for a healthy diet. A daily diet made up of reasonable quantities from each category will ensure a balanced consumption of essential nutrients to maintain health and energy without including unnecessary foods which add useless calories and lead to unwanted fat. A diet which follows these recommendations will encourage a healthy digestion, and constipation problems will become a thing of the past. No additional vitamin supplements will be necessary and of course the whole family will benefit from following this eating pattern.

Protein and minerals

A minimum of 6 oz of meat, fish, eggs or cheese should
be consumed daily.
½ pint skimmed milk should be consumed daily – max.
1 pint per day.

Fish	Any type	Steamed, grilled or microwaved without fat
Meat	Any type, lean cuts only	Grilled, roast or microwaved, without fat, and with all fat trimmed off before cooking, or trimmed afterwards
Poultry	Any type	Grilled, roast, microwaved, without fat. Do not eat any skin or fat
Offal	Any type	Steam, bake or microwave, without fat
Eggs		Cook in any way without the use of fat. Consume no more than 4 per week
Cheese	Preferably low fat e.g. Shape, Tendale, Edam	Restrict to 4 oz per week if possible
Cheese	Cottage	Unlimited quantities may be consumed
Yogurt	Any type	Unlimited

Vitamins
Approx. 12 oz of fruit or vegetables should be consumed daily

Vegetables	Any type	Unlimited, but always without butter
Fruit	Any type	Unlimited. Serve on its own, or with Shape Single or top of the milk or ice cream

Carbohydrates
A minimum of 4 oz to be consumed daily

Bread	Wholemeal or Crispbreads	Unlimited if eaten without fat; otherwise limit consumption to 3 slices of bread a day or 8 crispbreads
Cereal	Breakfast	1–2 oz per day
Rice	Brown	2 oz per day
Pasta	Fat free	Average portions 2–3 oz per day

Fats
Consume as little as possible

Low fat spread	Gold Outline	Maximum of ½ oz per day only. No butter or margarine
Cream	single	1–2 oz very occasionally

In addition, the following foods may be eaten in moderation

Milk puddings made with skimmed milk

Low-oil salad dressings, eg. Waistline or Weight Watchers

Cakes made without fat – see recipe (Apple Gâteau)

Ice cream

Pancakes made with skimmed milk

Yorkshire pudding made with skimmed milk in non-stick baking tin

Trifle made with only fatless sponge and custard made with skimmed milk, no cream

Cauliflower Cheese made with low-fat cheese and skimmed milk

Sausages, if grilled well

Nuts – only very few and avoid Brazils, Barcelona nuts or almonds

Horlicks, Ovaltine or Drinking Chocolate

Sauces if possible made with skimmed milk but *no* butter

Soups excepting cream soups

Soya, low fat type

Avoid the following foods
Butter, margarine, Flora, or similar products
Oil, lard, dripping, etc.
Soya, full fat type
Fried bread
Chapatis made with fat
Biscuits, all sweet varieties
Cakes, all except fat-free recipes
Milk, dried, whole
Cream, double, whipping, sterilized, canned.
Cheese, All types except Edam, Cottage, Tendale or
Shape Low Fat cheddar
Cheese spread
Quiches, Scotch eggs, cheese soufflé, Welsh Rarebit,
etc.
Fat from meat, streaky bacon
Skin from Chicken, turkey, duck, goose, etc.
Salami, Pâté, pork pie, meat pies, etc.
Sprats or Whitebait, fried
Fish plus oil
Anything fried, including mushrooms or onions
Dessicated coconut
Brazil nuts, almonds, Barcelona nuts
Chocolate, toffees, fudge, caramel, butterscotch
Mayonnaise
Marzipan
French Dressing made with oil
Pastries
Pork Scratchings

By referring to the list of foods and their fat content in the next chapter you will be able to see at a glance the amount of fat contained therein. Soon you will learn how to steer away from foods high in fat and will automatically select those that are low or even free from fat.

It is wise to restrict the consumption of fat in the long term. This will not only help to maintain your lower weight but it will also help the condition of your heart. Having said that, I have no wish to dampen the prospect of the future by saying that you can *never* eat any foods that are high in fat. Obviously if you attend a social function where there is little chance of avoiding a high-fat menu try to eat more of the foods that are low in fat and moderate the quantities of items saturated in fat. You can always cut down tomorrow so that the balance of intake can be levelled out again.

After I had followed the very low fat diet for my gall stone problem I found I really didn't want fatty food any more despite the fact that I was eventually told by my doctor that I could eat it without any ill effect. My gall stone problem now appears to have gone away but double cream and butter are just so rich I can't eat them and believe me, I never thought I would hear myself saying that! So basically I am saying that if you follow the reducing diet for a period of at least eight weeks your taste will have become adjusted to a low fat diet and the rest is easy. So please don't worry about finding enough willpower to restrict your intake of fat in the long term.

For some it is easier to have a set eating plan to follow, particularly after following a specified diet as set out in this book. Accordingly I have designed the following menu suggestions which have been added to the original diet. Keep an eye on your measurements and the scales and if you appear to be gaining weight cut down a little until you find the level of consumption that allows you to maintain your weight. *YOU* are the only one who can help ensure you maintain your goal. If you overeat you must cut down afterwards or alternatively you could cut down beforehand, in anticipation of a high fat meal.

Maintenance Programme

Eat three meals a day, selecting one meal from the Breakfast, Lunch and Dinner menus listed:

Daily allowance: 20 oz (1 pint) skimmed low fat milk

Breakfasts

1. Porridge made with water, served with milk from allowance and two teaspoons of honey or brown sugar. Plus 1 boiled egg and a thin slice (1 ounce) toast spread with a scraping of Gold or similar low-fat spread.
2. 5 prunes plus a natural yogurt, plus a slice of toast spread with a scraping of low fat spread and jam or marmalade.
3. Fruit compote, e.g. tinned grapefruit, oranges, peaches, pineapple, pears, etc. (6 ounces total), plus a poached egg on toast.
4. As much fresh fruit as you wish, any type, but eaten at one sitting, plus a slice of lean ham or 1 ounce toast spread with a scraping of low fat spread.
5. Tinned grapefruit in natural juice, plus 1 ounce toast, lightly spread with low fat spread and topped with a poached egg.
6. Fruit yogurt plus a slice of toast served with a small can of baked beans.
7. 1 ounce any cereal with a little sugar, and skimmed milk from allowance plus two pieces of fruit.
8. Slice of toast topped with 1 egg scrambled and a small can of tomatoes.

Lunches

1. Four or five pieces of any fresh fruit plus a yogurt.
2. Jacket potato topped with 8 ounces baked beans plus two pieces of any fresh fruit.
3. Jumbo sandwiches made with four slices of wholemeal bread thinly spread with Waistline or similar low calorie dressing, filled with salad and a little grated low fat cheese, plus two pieces of fresh fruit.
4. Two slices wholemeal toast with a large (16-ounce) can baked beans plus 2 pieces fresh fruit or a yogurt.
5. Rice salad: a bowl of chopped peppers, tomatoes, onion and cucumber mixed with cooked (boiled) brown rice and served with soy sauce, plus a skinless chicken joint.
6. Chicken joint (no skin) or prawns, served with a chopped salad of lettuce, cucumber, radish, spring onions, peppers, tomatoes, with soy sauce or yogurt dressing, or low oil dressing, e.g. Waistline, plus two pieces fresh fruit or a yogurt.
7. Jacket potato served with low fat cottage cheese or Shape Coleslaw, or a little Shape or Tendale low fat cheddar, plus Branston pickle and salad.
8. Six Ryvitas or similar crispbread with 4 ounces chicken (no skin) or 2 ounces lean ham, pork or beef with all fat removed, plus Branston pickle, two tomatoes and one piece of fruit.
9. Four Ryvitas spread with a scraping of Gold or Outline low fat spread, and topped with 2 ounces chicken, pork or beef (all lean) and Branston pickle, plus a piece of fruit.
10. Chicken joint (no skin), low fat yogurt and 8 ounces fresh fruit salad.
11. 4 ounces carton cottage cheese (any flavour) with six Ryvitas and a carton of Shape Coleslaw (4 ounces), tomato, lettuce and cucumber and carrot sticks.

12. 1-ounce slice wholemeal toast topped with 8-ounce can of baked beans plus one baked stuffed apple filled with 1 ounce dried fruit, a few breadcrumbs and sweetened with honey or artificial sweetener, and served with a plain yogurt.

13. Clear or vegetable soup, served with one slice of toast. Plus a chicken joint (no skin) and two pieces of fresh fruit.

14. Jacket potato with 2 ounces any meat or poultry (no fat or skin) served with Branston pickle and salad. Plus one piece of fruit.

15. Three slices of wholemeal bread made into open sandwiches with prawns and salad, dressed with low fat prawn cocktail dressing, plus one piece of fruit.

16. Jacket potato topped with chopped chicken, sweetcorn and peppers and a little Waistline reduced-oil dressing.

17. Two slices wholemeal toast with small tin baked beans and small tin of tomatoes, plus two pieces of fresh fruit.

18. 8-ounce carton low fat cottage cheese served with two tinned pear halves, chopped apple and celery, served on a bed of lettuce and garnished with tomato and cucumber, plus small serving of ice cream.

19. One-egg omelette filled with mushrooms cooked in stock, served with a large salad and a little reduced oil dressing.

20. Two slices toast spread with Gold or Outline and topped with asparagus spears.

Dinners

Select one from each section, i.e. a starter, main course and dessert.

Starters

1. Wedge of melon.
2. Half a grapefruit, sprinkled with sherry and brown sugar and grilled until gently browned.
3. Soup – any flavour but not a cream soup.
4. Grapefruit cocktail.
5. Seafood cocktail (with low fat dressing).
6. Prawn cocktail (with low fat dressing).
7. Pears filled with cottage cheese served on a bed of lettuce.
8. Garlic mushrooms (see recipe).
9. Stilton pears (see recipe).
10. Melon salad and hot herb loaf (see recipes).
11. Fruit sorbet.
12. French tomatoes (see recipe).
13. Stuffed mushrooms (see recipe).

Main courses

1. 8–10 ounces steamed, grilled or microwaved fish, any kind, served with unlimited vegetables, no butter.
2. 6–8 ounces chicken (no skin) cooked without fat and served with unlimited vegetables plus (if desired) a sauce made with skimmed milk, flavouring but no butter.
3. Chicken curry served with boiled brown rice (see recipe).
4. Trout, stuffed with prawns, cooked without butter and served with unlimited salad or vegetables.
5. Barbecued kebabs using any lean meat or poultry (see recipe for chicken kebabs). Served with boiled rice with additional vegetables if required.

6. Vegetable bake (see recipe) but add beans, lentils, etc., as desired and sprinkle a little grated low-fat cheese on the top.

7. Calves' or lamb's liver, braised with onions but without fat and served with unlimited vegetables.

8. Fish pie (see recipe) but add a little grated low-fat cheese with the fish and on top of the potato. Serve with unlimited vegetables.

9. Four Fish Fingers grilled or microwaved and served with unlimited vegetables.

10. 6 ounces grilled rump steak with all fat removed, served with jacket potato, peas, mushrooms and salad if desired.

11. 4 ounces lean lamb, served with dry roast parsnips, dry roast potatoes and other vegetables if desired.

12. 4 ounces roast leg of pork with all fat removed, served with apple sauce and unlimited vegetables.

13. 6 ounces roast duck (all skin removed) served with unlimited vegetables and a fat-free sauce, e.g. orange sauce, if desired.

14. 6 ounces roast turkey (no skin) served with cranberry sauce, dry roast potatoes and unlimited vegetables, plus chestnut stuffing and/or bread sauce made with skimmed milk and no butter.

15. 4 ounces grilled or baked gammon steak or gammon rashers, with all fat removed, served with pineapple and unlimited vegetables.

16. 3 ounces bacon, grilled and with all fat removed, served with one dry-fried egg, grilled tomatoes, baked beans and boiled or jacket potato.

17. Chicken joint baked or microwaved (no skin) in barbecue sauce (see recipe) and served with jacket potato or boiled brown rice plus vegetables of your choice.

18. Prawn or chicken Chop Suey (see recipe) plus other Chinese vegetables and boiled brown rice.

19. Baked chicken joint (no skin) plus stuffed mushrooms (see recipe) and unlimited vegetables.

20. 4 ounces roast beef (no fat), dry roast potatoes, one small Yorkshire pudding made with skimmed milk in a non-stick baking tin, plus unlimited vegetables and a little horseradish sauce if desired.

Desserts
1. Fresh fruit salad plus a little Shape Single.
2. One banana sliced in two lengthways and served with one scoop ice cream, topped with raspberry sauce.
3. Stuffed apple (see recipe) served with a little Shape Single or top of the milk.
4. Strawberries served with one scoop ice cream or with Shape Single.
5. Raspberries served with one scoop ice cream.
6. Pears cooked in red wine (see recipe) and served with a little Shape Single.
7. Oranges in Cointreau (see recipe) served with a little Shape Single.
8. Pineapple in Kirsch (see recipe) served with ice cream.
9. Sliced banana topped with fresh raspberries and ice cream.
10. Fresh peaches sliced and served with fresh raspberries and a scoop of ice cream.
11. Any two pieces of fresh fruit plus a yogurt.
12. Fruit sorbet, any flavour plus a scoop of ice cream if desired.
13. Meringue basket filled with raspberries or strawberries and topped with a teaspoon of Shape Double.
14. Pears in meringue (see recipe), served with a little Shape Single.
15. Green figs plus a little Shape Single.
16. Small slice Apple Gâteau (see recipe).

10
Food index

The following food index lists the fat content of almost all everyday foods and has been designed in such a way that you can see the fat content of food at a glance.

As a simple guide to those following the weight/inch loss diet described in Chapter 5, any foods may be selected and eaten freely if they contain virtually no fat. Alcohol of course has no fat but as it is high in calories its consumption should be moderated.

For those who have successfully lost all excess weight and inches and are using the maintenance programme, attempt to select foods with less than 4 grams of fat per ounce.

The food tables have been drawn up to indicate the fat content of 25 grams of each item listed and for the sake of convenience I have taken 25 grams to equal 1 oz. (In actual fact there are a little over 28 grams per ounce.) The reason for this is that most products are labelled with the composition per 100 grams and my tables are therefore based on a quarter of this value.

By looking through these tables you will be able to learn quickly which foods are high and which are low in fat and after a while you will be able to steer an easy course to healthy eating and a long and active life.

● negligible ○ zero

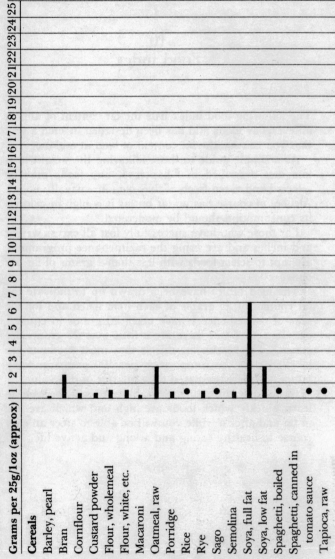

Grams per 25g/1oz (approx)	1	2	3	4	5	6	7	8	9	10	11	12	13	14	15	16	17	18	19	20	21	22	23	24	25

Cereals

Barley, pearl
Bran
Cornflour
Custard powder
Flour, wholemeal
Flour, white, etc.
Macaroni
Oatmeal, raw
Porridge
Rice
Rye
Sago
Semolina
Soya, full fat
Soya, low fat
Spaghetti, boiled
Spaghetti, canned in tomato sauce
Tapioca, raw

Wholemeal, brown,
hovis, white
Fried
Fruit loaf, malt
Rolls, crusty
Rolls, soft
Chapatis, with fat
Chapatis, without fat

Breakfast cereals
All Bran
Cornflakes
Grapenuts
Muesli
Puffed Wheat
Ready Brek
Rice Krispies
Shredded Wheat
Special K
Sugar Puffs
Weetabix

● negligible ○ zero

Grams per 25g/1oz (approx) | 1 2 3 4 5 6 7 8 9 10 11 12 13 14 15 16 17 18 19 20 21 22 23 24 25

Biscuits

Chocolate, full coated

Cream biscuits

Cream crackers

Crispbread, rye

Crispbread, wheat starch reduced

Digestive, plain

Digestive, chocolate

Ginger nuts

Matzo

Oatcakes

Semi-sweet

Short-sweet

Shortbread

Wafers, filled

Water biscuits

Cakes

Fancy, iced

Gingerbread
Madeira
Rock
Sponge, with fat
Sponge, without fat

Buns and pastries
Currant buns
Doughnuts
Eclairs
Jam tarts
Mince pies
Pastry, choux
Pastry, flaky
Pastry, shortcrust
Scones
Scotch pancakes

Puddings
Apple crumble
Bread & butter pudding

● negligible ○ zero

Grams per 25g/1oz (approx)	1	2	3	4	5	6	7	8	9	10	11	12	13	14	15	16	17	18	19	20	21	22	23	24	25
Cheesecake																									
Christmas pudding																									
Egg custard																									
Custard tart																									
Dumpling																									
Fruit pie, pastry top and bottom																									
Fruit pie, pastry top only																									
Ice cream, dairy																									
Ice cream, non-dairy																									
Jelly	○																								
Lemon meringue pie																									
Meringues	○																								
Milk puddings																									
Rice, canned																									
Pancakes																									
Queen of puddings																									
Sponge pudding																									
Suet pudding																									
Treacle tart																									

Milk and milk products
Milk, cows':
  Fresh, whole
  Channel Isles
  Sterilised
  Longlife, UHT treated
  Fresh, skimmed
  Condensed, whole
  Condensed, skimmed
  Evaporated, whole
  Dried, whole
  Dried, skimmed
Milk, goats'
Butter
Gold
Cream, single
Cream, double
Cream, whipping
Shape, single
Shape, double

● negligible ○ zero

Grams per 25g/1oz (approx)	1 2 3 4 5 6 7 8 9 10 11 12 13 14 15 16 17 18 19 20 21 22 23 24 25
Cream, sterilised canned	6
Cheese:	
Camembert	6
Cheddar	8
Shape Cheddar	4
Danish Blue	7
Edam	5
Parmesan	7
Stilton	9
Cottage, with cream	1
Cottage, without cream	●
Cream Cheese	12
Shape, soft	2
Processed, cream	6
Cheese spread	5
Yogurt (low fat):	
Natural	●
Flavoured	●
Fruit	●
Hazelnut	

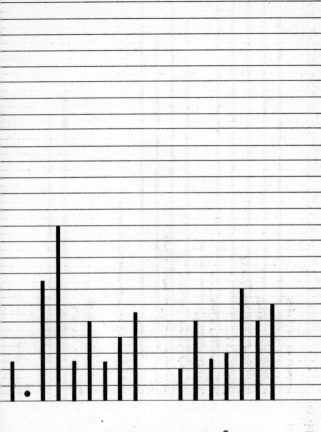

Whole, raw
White only
Yolk only
Dried
Boiled
Fried
Poached
Omelette
Scrambled

Egg and cheese dishes
Cauliflower cheese
Cheese souffle
Macaroni cheese
Pizza, cheese and tomato
Quiche Lorraine
Scotch egg
Welsh rarebit

● negligible ○ zero

Grams per 25g/1oz (approx)	1	2	3	4	5	6	7	8	9	10	11	12	13	14	15	16	17	18	19	20	21	22	23	24	25

Fats and oils

Butter																						▮			
Cod liver oil																									▮
Compound cooking fat																									▮
Dripping, beef																									▮
Lard																									▮
Low fat spread (e.g. Gold)									▮																
Margarine, all kinds																					▮				
Suet, block																									▮
Suet, shredded																							▮		
Vegetable oils																									▮

Meat and meat products

Bacon

Lean, raw		▮																							
Fat, raw																				▮					
Fat, cooked																		▮							
Collar joint:																									
Raw, lean and fat							▮																		
Boiled, lean and fat						▮																			

Raw, lean and fat
Boiled, lean and fat
Boiled, lean only
Gammon rashers:
    Grilled, lean and fat
    Grilled, lean only
Rashers, fried:
    Lean only
    Back, lean and fat
    Middle, lean and fat
    Streaky, lean and fat
Rashers, grilled:
    Lean only
    Back, lean and fat
    Middle, lean and fat
    Streaky, lean and fat

Beef
Brisket: boiled, lean and fat
Forerib roast:
    Lean and fat

● negligible ○ zero

Grams per 25g/1oz (approx)	1	2	3	4	5	6	7	8	9	10	11	12	13	14	15	16	17	18	19	20	21	22	23	24	25
Forerib roast:																									
Lean only			▮																						
Mince:																									
Raw				▮																					
Stewed				▮																					
Rump steak, fried:																									
Lean and fat				▮																					
Lean only		▮																							
Rump steak, grilled:																									
Lean and fat			▮																						
Lean only		▮																							
Silverside, salted and boiled:																									
Lean and fat			▮																						
Lean only	▮																								
Sirloin, roast or grilled:																									
Lean and fat					▮																				
Lean only			▮																						
Stewing steak:																									
Stewed, lean and fat			▮																						
Topside roast:																									

Lamb

Breast, roast:
Lean and fat
Lean only

Chops, loin, grilled:
Lean and fat
Lean and fat, weighed
with bone
Lean only
Lean only, weighed
with bone

Cutlets, grilled:
Lean and fat
Lean and fat, weighed
with bone
Lean only
Lean only, weighed
with bone

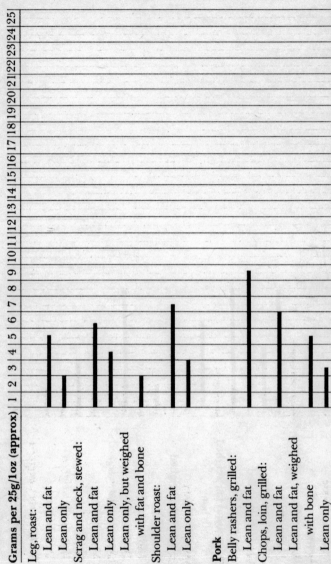

● negligible ○ zero

Grams per 25g/1oz (approx)	1	2	3	4	5	6	7	8	9	10	11	12	13	14	15	16	17	18	19	20	21	22	23	24	25

Leg, roast:
Lean and fat
Lean only

Scrag and neck, stewed:
Lean and fat
Lean only
Lean only, but weighed
with fat and bone

Shoulder roast:
Lean and fat
Lean only

Pork

Belly rashers, grilled:
Lean and fat

Chops, loin, grilled:
Lean and fat
Lean and fat, weighed
with bone
Lean only

fat and bone
Leg roast:
    Lean and fat
    Lean only

Veal
Cutlet, fried
Fillet, roast

Poultry and game
Chicken, boiled:
    Meat only
    Light meat
    Dark meat
Chicken, roast:
    Meat only
    Meat and skin
    Light meat
    Dark meat
Wing quarter, weighed
    with bone

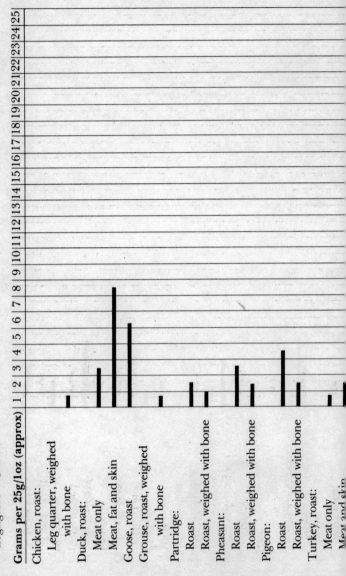

● negligible ○ zero

Grams per 25g/1oz (approx) | 1 | 2 | 3 | 4 | 5 | 6 | 7 | 8 | 9 | 10 | 11 | 12 | 13 | 14 | 15 | 16 | 17 | 18 | 19 | 20 | 21 | 22 | 23 | 24 | 25

Chicken, roast:
  Leg quarter, weighed
    with bone
Duck, roast:
  Meat only
  Meat, fat and skin
Goose, roast
Grouse, roast, weighed
    with bone
Partridge:
  Roast
  Roast, weighed with bone
Pheasant:
  Roast
  Roast, weighed with bone
Pigeon:
  Roast
  Roast, weighed with bone
Turkey, roast:
  Meat only
  Meat and skin

Dark meat

Hare:
Stewed
Stewed, weighed
with bone

Rabbit:
Stewed
Stewed, weighed
with bone

Venison, roast

Offal
Brain:
Calf, boiled
Lamb, boiled

Heart:
Sheep, roast
Ox, stewed

Kidney:
Lamb, fried
Ox, stewed

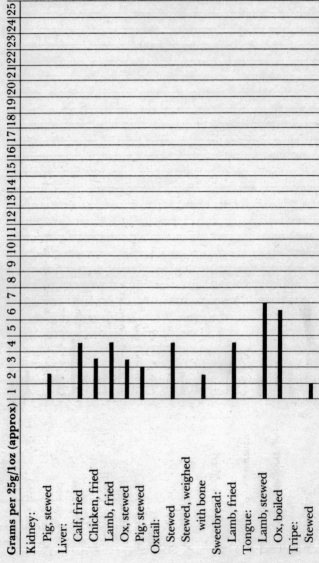

● negligible ○ zero

Grams per 25g/1oz (approx)	1	2	3	4	5	6	7	8	9	10	11	12	13	14	15	16	17	18	19	20	21	22	23	24	25

Kidney:
Pig, stewed

Liver:
Calf, fried
Chicken, fried
Lamb, fried
Ox, stewed
Pig, stewed

Oxtail:
Stewed
Stewed, weighed
with bone

Sweetbread:
Lamb, fried

Tongue:
Lamb, stewed
Ox, boiled

Tripe:
Stewed

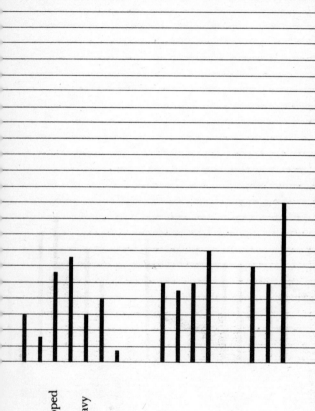

Canned meats
Corned beef
Ham
Ham and pork, chopped
Luncheon meat
Stewed steak with gravy
Tongue
Veal, jellied

Offal products
Black pudding, fried
Faggots
Haggis, boiled
Liver sausage

Sausages
Frankfurters
Polony
Salami

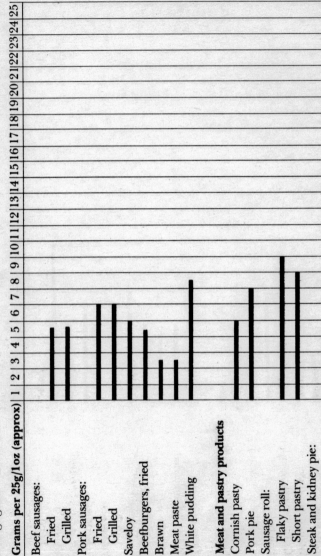

● negligible   ○ zero

Grams per 25g/1oz (approx) | 1 | 2 | 3 | 4 | 5 | 6 | 7 | 8 | 9 | 10 | 11 | 12 | 13 | 14 | 15 | 16 | 17 | 18 | 19 | 20 | 21 | 22 | 23 | 24 | 25

Beef sausages:
  Fried
  Grilled
Pork sausages:
  Fried
  Grilled
Saveloy
Beefburgers, fried
Brawn
Meat paste
White pudding

Meat and pastry products
Cornish pasty
Pork pie
Sausage roll:
  Flaky pastry
  Short pastry
Steak and kidney pie:
  Pastry top only

Beef steak pudding

Beef stew

Bolognese sauce

Curried meat

Hot pot

Irish stew

Moussaka

Shepherd's pie

Fish

White fish

Cod:

Baked

Fried in batter

Grilled

Poached

Steamed

Smoked, poached

Haddock:

Fried

Steamed

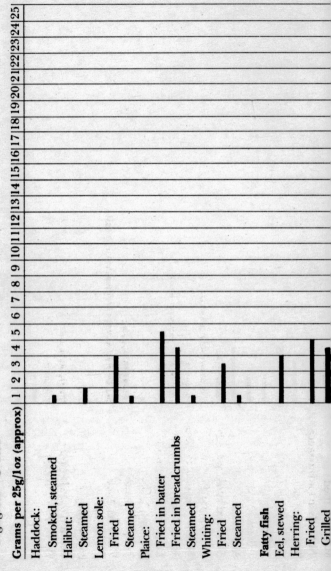

● negligible ○ zero

Grams per 25g/1oz (approx) | 1 | 2 | 3 | 4 | 5 | 6 | 7 | 8 | 9 | 10 | 11 | 12 | 13 | 14 | 15 | 16 | 17 | 18 | 19 | 20 | 21 | 22 | 23 | 24 | 25

Haddock:
  Smoked, steamed

Halibut:
  Steamed

Lemon sole:
  Fried
  Steamed

Plaice:
  Fried in batter
  Fried in breadcrumbs
  Steamed

Whiting:
  Fried
  Steamed

Fatty fish
Eel, stewed
Herring:
  Fried
  Grilled

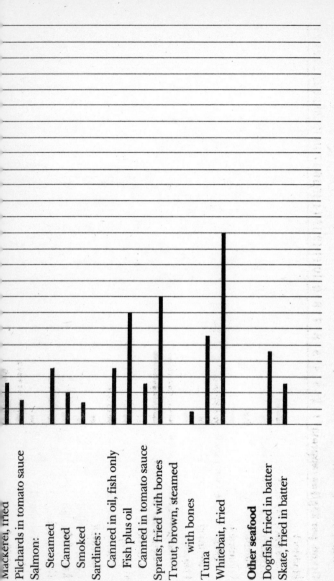

Mackerel, fried
Pilchards in tomato sauce

Salmon:
  Steamed
  Canned
  Smoked

Sardines:
  Canned in oil, fish only
  Fish plus oil
  Canned in tomato sauce

Sprats, fried with bones

Trout, brown, steamed
  with bones

Tuna

Whitebait, fried

Other seafood
Dogfish, fried in batter
Skate, fried in batter

● negligible ○ zero

Grams per 25g/1oz (approx)	1	2	3	4	5	6	7	8	9	10	11	12	13	14	15	16	17	18	19	20	21	22	23	24	25

Crab:
Boiled
Boiled, weighed with shell

Lobster:
Boiled
Boiled, weighed with shell

Prawns:
Boiled
Boiled, weighed with shell

Scampi, fried

Shrimps:
Boiled
Boiled with shells
Canned

Cockles, boiled
Mussels, boiled
Oysters, raw
Scallops, steamed
Whelks, boiled
Winkles

Fish cakes, fried
Fish fingers, fried
Fish paste
Fish pie
Kedgeree
Roe:

Cod, hard, fried
Herring, soft, fried

Vegetables
Ackee, canned
Artichokes:
  Globe, boiled
  Jerusalem, boiled
Asparagus
Aubergine
Avocado
Beans:
  French
  Runner
  Broad

● negligible ○ zero

Grams per 25g/1oz (approx)	1	2	3	4	5	6	7	8	9	10	11	12	13	14	15	16	17	18	19	20	21	22	23	24	25
Beans:																									
Butter	●																								
Haricot	●																								
Baked, canned in tomato sauce		●																							
Mung, green, cooked	●																								
Red kidney	▌																								
Bean sprouts	●																								
Beetroot	●																								
Broccoli tops	●																								
Brussels sprouts	●																								
Cabbage:																									
Red	●																								
Savoy	●																								
Spring	●																								
White	●																								
Winter	●																								
Carrots	●																								
Cauliflower	●																								

Chicory
Cucumber
Horseradish
Laverbread
Leeks
Lentils, raw
Masar dahl, cooked
Lettuce
Marrow
Mushrooms, raw
Mushrooms, fried
Mustard and cress
Okra
Onions, all except fried
Onions, fried
Parsley
Parsnips
Peas, all kinds
Chick peas:
Bengal, cooked dahl
Channa, dahl

● negligible ○ zero

Grams per 25g/1oz (approx)	Value
Peppers, green	● (negligible)
Plantain:	
Green, boiled	● (negligible)
Ripe, fried	3
Potatoes:	
Boiled, baked with/without skins, no fat	● (negligible)
Roast	1.5
Chips, average, home made	3
Chips, frozen, fried	5
Crisps	9
Pumpkin	● (negligible)
Radishes	● (negligible)
Salsify	● (negligible)
Seakale	● (negligible)
Spinach	● (negligible)
Spring greens	● (negligible)
Swedes	● (negligible)
Sweetcorn	● (negligible)

Scale: 1 2 3 4 5 6 7 8 9 10 11 12 13 14 15 16 17 18 19 20 21 22 23 24 25

Tomatoes
Tomatoes, fried
Turnips
Watercress
Yam

Fruit
Apples
Apricots
Avocado pears
Bananas
Bilberries
Blackberries
Cherries
Cranberries
Currants
Damsons
Dates
Figs
Fruit pie filling
Fruit salad
Gooseberries

● negligible ○ zero

Grams per 25g/1oz (approx)	1	2	3	4	5	6	7	8	9	10	11	12	13	14	15	16	17	18	19	20	21	22	23	24	25
Grapes	●																								
Grapefruit	●																								
Greengages	●																								
Guavas	●																								
Lemons	●																								
Loganberries	●																								
Lychees	●																								
Mandarin oranges	●																								
Mangoes	●																								
Medlars	●																								
Melons	●																								
Mulberries	●																								
Nectarines	●																								
Olives																									
Oranges	●																								
Passion fruit	●																								
Paw paw	●																								
Peaches	●																								
Pears	●																								
Pineapple	●																								
Plums	●																								

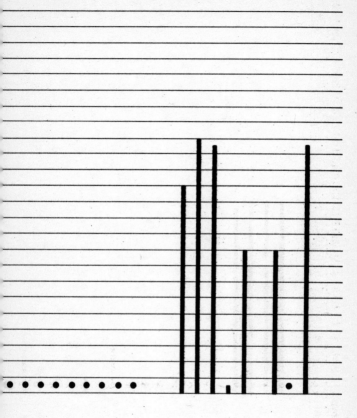

Pomegranate
Prunes
Quinces
Raisins
Raspberries
Rhubarb
Strawberries
Sultanas
Tangerines

Nuts
Almonds
Barcelona
Brazil
Chestnuts
Cob or hazel
Coconut:
Fresh
Milk
Desiccated

● negligible ○ zero

Grams per 25g/1oz (approx)

	1	2	3	4	5	6	7	8	9	10	11	12	13	14	15	16	17	18	19	20	21	22	23	24	25

Peanuts:

Fresh	████████████
Roasted and salted	████████████
Peanut butter	████████████
Walnuts	███████████

Sugars and preserves

Sugars:

Glucose liquid	○
Sugar, all	○
Syrup	○
Treacle	○

Preserves:

Cherries, glace	○
Honeycomb	█
Honey in jars	● ○
Jam	██
Lemon curd, starch based	███
Lemon curd, home made	○
Marmalade	

Mincemeat

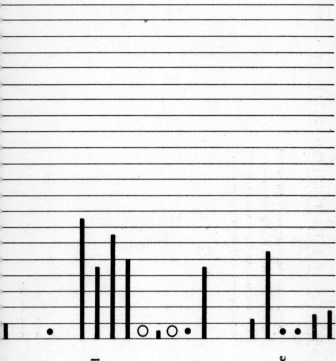

Confectionery
Boiled sweets
Chocolate, average,
plain or milk
Chocolate, fancy and filled
Bounty Bar
Mars Bar
Fruit Gums
Liquorice
Pastilles
Peppermints
Toffees

Beverages
Bournvita
Cocoa powder
Coffee and chicory essence
Coffee
Drinking chocolate
Horlicks

• negligible ○ zero

Grams per 25g/1oz (approx)	1	2	3	4	5	6	7	8	9	10	11	12	13	14	15	16	17	18	19	20	21	22	23	24	25
Ovaltine	▮																								
Tea	•																								
Soft drinks																									
Coca Cola	○																								
Grapefruit juice	•																								
Lemonade	○																								
Lime juice cordial	○																								
Lucozade	○																								
Orange drink	○																								
Orange juice	•																								
Pineapple juice	•																								
Ribena	○																								
Rosehip syrup	○																								
Tomato juice	•																								
Beers																									
Brown ale	•																								
Canned beer	•																								
Draught	•																								
Keg	•																								

Pale ale	●
Stout	●
Stout, extra	●
Strong ale	●
Ciders	
All types	○
Wines	
All types	○
Wines, fortified	
Port	○
Sherry	○
Vermouths	
All types	○
Liqueurs	
Advocaat	│
Cherry brandy	○
Curaçao	○

● negligible ○ zero

Grams per 25g/1oz (approx)	1	2	3	4	5	6	7	8	9	10	11	12	13	14	15	16	17	18	19	20	21	22	23	24	25

Spirits
All types ○

Sauces and pickles
Bread sauce
Brown sauce ●
Cheese sauce
Chutney ●
French dressing
Mayonnaise
Onion sauce ●
Piccalilli ●
Pickle, sweet
Salad cream
Waistline
Tomato ketchup ●
Tomato puree ●
Tomato sauce
White sauce:
  Savoury
  Sweet

Bone and vegetable broth
Chicken, cream of:
  Ready to serve
  Condensed
  Condensed, as served
Chicken noodle
Lentil
Minestrone
Mushroom, cream of
Oxtail
Tomato, cream of:
  Ready to serve
  Condensed
  Condensed, as served
Vegetable

Miscellaneous
Baking powder
Bovril
Coleslaw, Shape
Coleslaw, normal

● negligible   ○ zero

Grams per 25g/1oz (approx) 1 2 3 4 5 6 7 8 9 10 11 12 13 14 15 16 17 18 19 20 21 22 23 24 25

Curry powder
Gelatine
Ginger, ground
Marmite
Oxo cubes
Mustard powder
Pepper
Salt
Vinegar
Yeast, bakers
Yeast, dried

11
Note to cholesterol patients

The low fat diet described in this book will certainly help those who suffer from high cholesterol, but some foods whilst low in fat are actually very high in cholesterol and it is for this reason that I am listing the following foods.

Anyone who has a high-cholesterol problem should avoid the following foods:

Eggs, egg dishes, Scotch eggs
Offal: Brain, heart, kidney, liver, sweetbread, tongue, liver sausage pâté
Duck, dark meat of chicken or turkey, steak and kidney pie, lamb, pork, salami
Fish roe, kedgeree, whiting, sardines, mackerel, taramasalata
Butter, margarine, cream, cheese, suet
Pastry, cakes, biscuits, buns
Seafood including crab, lobster, prawns, scampi, shrimps, mussels, whelks, winkles
Nuts including peanuts, cashews
Avocado pears, olives
Mayonnaise, salad cream
Chocolate, crisps
Coconut and coconut oil
Lemon curd

The following are excerpts from just a few of the many readers' letters written to Rosemary Conley after publication of her *Hip and Thigh Diet*:

'After just 4 weeks I have achieved incredible results! I am absolutely delighted and amazed. I have never achieved such good results before.'
Mrs L. G., Northumberland

'I never thought I'd be writing to anyone saying "your diet is wonderful" but it is and I am!'
Mrs C. W., Middlesex

'I have been following your diet for three weeks and so far have lost 13 lbs. I have followed many diets over the last 10 years. Never have I lost so much so easily and quickly.'
Mrs B. J., Lincolnshire

'Your *Hip and Thigh Diet* has completely changed my life. . . I look 10 years younger and it's all thanks to you. . . I seem to have so much more confidence since regaining my teenage figure! I am so grateful.'
Mrs V. C., South Humberside

'My measurements used to be 36″, 28″, 38″ and my new measurements are 36″ (no loss there I'm glad to say), 26″, 34″ – but what is more important is that the FAT seems to have disappeared. I have been measuring my thighs, knees and upper arms and those measurements used to be 22½″, 16″ and 12″ respectively. Now my thighs, knees and arms are 20″, 14″ and 10½″. Wonderful! Everything fits like a dream. . . My husband can't believe it. He says I look just like I did when we got married nearly 18 years ago and is just as thrilled as I am with my new shape. . . I have attempted diets before like millions of women but never achieved the shape I wanted. Now I have, and I would just like to thank you for sharing your experience with myself and others.'
Mrs S. A., Wiltshire